The New Birth

The New Birth

A HANDBOOK OF
SCRIPTUAL DOCUMENTATION

by
CYRIL A. CRICHLOW

PAGEANT PRESS, INC. • NEW YORK

Dedicated to My Wife

CAROLINE MAY CRICHLOW

*whose unfailing loyalty, cooperation and faith have been my
constant inspiration*

A BIBLE STUDY IN
SPIRITUAL BIOLOGY
(A Handbook)

Presenting Some New Aspects
— Covering a New Approach
— Leading to New Light
— On an Age-old but Vital Subject

And Further Evidencing that Christian Worship Divinely
Rests on the Principle of Sex and that, Like Other World
Religions of the Past, Its Essential Structure is Based on
Phallic Symbolism

Contents

III

BEGOTTEN AGAIN AND BEGETTAL COMPLETED

IV

THE MESSIANIC KINGDOM ESTABLISHED & THE LIFE HEREAFTER

V

APPENDICES

Acknowledgment

AS HEREWITH PRESENTED AND DELINEATED BY THE WRITER through a combined missionary experience and correspondence extended over the years, this handbook is the outgrowth of numerous suggestions on the part of interested friends to have the subject matter of *The New Birth* with its novel approach treated a little more comprehensively and put in more permanent arrangement and form.

It is therefore trusted that its printing, as now effected, will lead to the opening of many eyes to an understanding of its critical importance and thus prove a source of inspiration and a wellspring of blessing to all who take time to ponder its vital message and give it their best and most concentrated and undivided attention.

Acknowledgment is now given to those who have generously and unstintingly stood by us in the present endeavors, which have been a joy although accompanied by a lot of heartaches. Our heartfelt thanks therefore go out to the many beneficiaries of its message who have rallied to our assistance with their moral support and financial backing.

Jesus saith unto Nicodemus: "Marvel not that I said unto thee, *Ye must be BEGOTTEN AGAIN!*"   —John 3:7

"Then said He unto His disciples, Therefore, every scribe which is instructed unto the Kingdom of the *Heavens* [Gr. plural] is like unto a man that is an householder, which bringeth forth out of his treasure things new and old."
            —Matthew 13:52.

Thematic Development

THE SUBJECT MATTER OF *The New Birth* MAY BE BROKEN down to these four broad outlines:

As related to Spiritual Biology, we have the pith of this aspect compactly summed up in the following commentary by a nationally famous theologian, which gives us the cue to its true definition and correct explanation. Having John 3:3-6 very definitely in mind, he states:

> "In the Christian order, as in the scientific, there is no spontaneous generation: Life must come from life; God-Life must come from God. Hence, as the soul is the life of the body, so the God-Life is the life of the soul. There is no such thing as a man becoming more and more generous, less and less selfish, and then suddenly finding himself a partaker of the Divine Life. The sea shell cannot grow and grow until it becomes an elephant. As Our Lord said: 'Unless you are BORN AGAIN. . . .'"

The point is, it takes life to beget life, to begin with. In addition, it also takes *like* to beget *like*, this being from the beginning of time (*sui generis*) the inflexible divine law and order of creation—hence "every living creature after its own kind: and it was so."—Genesis 1:24. Therefore, in the Christian order, Christ must beget the likeness of Himself in the believer, which becomes his regeneration; and in the totality and completeness of this divine operation, it follows that Christ must Himself beget or otherwise proliferate manifold Christs, or images, which become identified with Him organically and spiritually as THE BODY OF CHRIST, even as the vine and its branches. This is the essence of Spiritual Biology.

Needless to say, without the intromission from above of the divine sperm to spark initially a new life into being—conditioned with all necessary celestial characteristics and attributes as well as appropriate functions for celestial existence, which constitutes the Life Hereafter—and thus literally to generate and produce an entirely *new creature in Christ Jesus,* there can be no begettal of the believer into the Kingdom of God. In other words, there can be no Christian salvation into heaven without the New Birth, which in the final analysis exactly focuses those compelling and atom-splitting words of the Master: *"Ye must be begotten again!"*

And thus, in a nutshell, our thesis is the elaboration of a theme which is quite concisely summed up by Pastor David Nield of Wellington, New Zealand, in the following considered analysis. Writing in *Begotten Again or Born Again—Which?*, published around 1915, he has this to say:

"We are 'waiting for sonship' (Romans 8:23), therefore not born. When I make the statement that the New Birth takes place at the resurrection, I do not mean that we cannot have our sins forgiven (at least conditionally) until the second coming of Christ. I do not mean that the believer is not created anew in Christ Jesus unto good works until Christ comes. I do not mean that the believer may not enjoy and possess the love of God which passeth understanding, nor do I mean that he cannot be filled with the Holy Spirit until he is raised from the dead at the second coming of Christ.

"But I do mean that unless we have been converted, and kept converted, and possess a knowledge of our sins forgiven, and enjoy the peace and love of God, and have the Spirit of Christ dwelling in us in this life before the second coming of Christ, then we are none of His, and we shall never be born again or attain unto the resurrection from among the dead. I mean that the change of condition at conversion is not either properly or scripturally defined by the term 'born again'; but it is by the word 'begotten' . . . *When we understand that conversion is best understood as CONCEPTION or BEGETTAL, then we have harmony throughout all the Scriptures as to the time when the New Birth takes place.*"

The real crux of the present Study becomes apparent when the reader has gotten past the topics under "The Divine Backdrop". The historical, dispensational, and other related Scriptural aspects, are the necessary hurdles which every serious student of the Word of God has to buck and must consequently with great patience take in his stride. For it is this part of the thematic scheme which provides the divine setting and perspective for what comes after, and underscores the correct approach to the subject and treatment of *The New Birth*.

"The danger of man's right to knowledge comes not from those who are ignorant and know it, but from those who have been allowed to learn only one set of facts and one interpretation of them. They are ignorant and do not know it."

—*Dr. Grayson L. Kirk*
President of Columbia University

Preface

FOR THOSE DESIRING A PRELIMINARY PROSPECTUS OF *The New Birth*, special attention must be called to "Summary Digest" and to "Inception and Background" in the Appendix to this Bible study, which give an immediate preview together with the necessary insight.

Being a Bible study and hence making no other pretense, scriptural references will be found abounding freely throughout the various topics, which makes a word of caution seem urgently necessary at this point.

And this brings us to the instant recognition that, while by itself not the conclusive factor or absolute determinant of the correctness of divine truth as humanly conceived and presented, the reasoning involved should at least have the merit of resting on a pattern of *sound words*—that is to say, in the spirit and not necessarily in the letter—in order to evidence some semblance of scriptural justification and support therefor. Nevertheless, of this we have to be constantly reminded: that, far from exclusively relying on mere assertion, hypothesis or dogmatic treatment, every biblical interpreter and writer tries to rest his case on the amassing of scriptural texts and citations which more or less strengthen his own position or otherwise help to demolish and overthrow his opposition.

In the final analysis, we can be sure that "the letter killeth, but the spirit giveth life." This is hard for many biblical expositors and experts to accept or grant, of course. Hence, the only safety lies in following "the Mind of Christ" as it is unqualifiedly expressed in the revelation of the *Holy Spirit Himself* communicated directly in the believer's heart —in other words, *"the Witness of God!"* This alone, from the fact that it is both internal and personal, is the indispensable ingredient every zealous Bible student must have in his quest for truth, and which alone can establish for him, and to his own personal satisfaction, its correctness or falsity. Like the woman *enceinte,* the man who is begotten initially and thereafter is divinely quickened *knows* it beyond shadow of doubt. No amount of frenzied disputation and sophistry can take away from him that knowledge—this being infallibly *"the Witness of God!"*

Only the Living Christ as He personally abides within— who thereby manifests Himself as the Indwelling Presence which expresses THE HOLY SPIRIT, this truly being in turn His Divine *alter ego*—can bring correction, reproof, enlightenment, certain and exact knowledge of the truth, and even invincible belief to those who with hungry hearts in prayerful attitude seek to know of the doctrine of Christ. (See John 7:17; 16:7-15; 4:23, 24; II Corinthians 3:6; and I John 5:9, 10.)

Further, the reader will observe that, *as a study,* the format seemingly involves two opposite procedures or methods: namely, compression and expansion. The former is seen in the interpretive treatment given to the various scriptural passages under consideration, with its bracketed interpolations and running commentary style; and the latter expressed in the terms of constant repetition and emphasis as the theme from topic to topic gradually builds up to a climax, which the very nature of a study requires. Either way, carping criticism is sure to find what it wants—an open season, a grand field day, and happy hunting.

In a recent article on "John Marshall—Our 'Greatest Dissenter',"* Edmond Cahn (Professor of Law at New York

---

* *New York (Sunday) Times* Magazine Section, August 21, 1955. Reprinted by permission of author.

University) illuminated his subject with the following sage
observation.

"If the Federalist party lost elections," he wrote, "Marshall at least won the constitutional arguments. No one could
have been better endowed to express and defend an unpopular doctrine. Free as he was of the cumbersome paraphernalia of technical learning, he virtually never became en-
tangled in ancient precedents. No American jurist has been
less bound by the past.

"He seems to have followed two main policies: (1) Identify the exact goal of your reasoning, start your exposition
very far away from it, get your adversary to admit to some
apparently self-evident and innocuous proposition, and then
move step by step from there to the goal, never relaxing your
show of absolute, inevitable certitude. (2) Among reason-
able men 'yes' is to be said briefly, 'no' is to be said at length.

"In a republic, therefore, unpopular decisions should be
very elaborate and prolix, thus showing that every possible
objection has been considered and that the unpopular outcome is logically inescapable. Hence, let there be a flood of
words. Nevertheless, it is helpful to drop a quotable legal
aphorism here and there in the verbal sea, for use as a buoy
or life raft.

"These were Marshall's talents. With them he undertook
a seemingly hopeless resistance to the current of his times."

The foregoing reflects accurately the pattern followed
in the writer's presentation of *The New Birth*. The methods
of pedagogy are very simple, as every schoolteacher under-
stands—*repeat everlastingly!* And this is the method the
author has used in the treatment of the subject.

Constant repetition is the pedagogical backbone and the
effective routine of the successful teacher, especially where
new, difficult, and otherwise unusual subjects and approaches in the curriculum are being handled and presented
for the first time. *The point is to drive the lesson and its
meaning home!*

In other words, that the unusual and the difficult and the new have to be stated at quite some length, even at the risk of being redundant and prolix and, of course, saying the same things over and over again, is the only excuse for the format, treatment, and style of the writer, who thus bespeaks the sympathetic consideration of all men of goodwill, "especially those of the household of faith."—Galatians 6:10.

Moreover, in Proverbs 4:18 we read that "the path of the just is as the shining light that shineth more and more unto the perfect day." Accordingly, it need hardly be stated at this juncture that the eternal light that beckons is always progressive, being apprehended only a little at a time and a day's march at a time and never in its divine entirety. Hence there is always more and more over the horizon of infinity, as the search for certainty and truth leads ever onwards.

Thus man finds himself hopelessly circumscribed and his finite understanding of things divine constantly limited, and in the process of seeking he learns, perhaps the painful way, that he can never really touch bottom in God's infinite sea of wisdom and salvation.

The only significance to be given the present attempt is the sincere desire to be helpful spiritually—to open the subject, first of all; next to awaken interest and thus spur the intellect and quicken the heart; to present some of the highlights as well as some of the evident pitfalls to be found wherever doubts assail and questions arise, being thereby indicative of the fact that there is much room for honest differences; and lastly, to suggest leads, either constructively or directly, that could result in the making of one's own separate investigations and that conceivably could bring about quite different answers and conclusions from those presented. Needless to say, the whole cause of Christian freedom, progress, and discovery will be enormously served thereby.

The author has tried hard not to seem too insufferably dogmatic, although about this some may disagree and think otherwise. Nonetheless, bigotry and pharisaism are not by any remote chance a part of his spiritual make-up and system. His presentation simply reflects, as it is intended to, his own personal persuasion and convictions, to which he has been graciously guided by *the unquenchable flaming Witness within* and by his own deep enthusiasm and confidence —that's all.

And further deponent sayeth not!

CYRIL A. CRICHLOW

Washington, D.C., U.S.A.,
September 12, 1955.

"Here's freedom to him that wad write,
Here's freedom to him that wad read!
There's none ever feared
That the truth should be heered,
But they whom the truth wad indict."

I

The Divine Backdrop

1. "Begotten" and "Born" Distinguished

THE GREEK ORIGINAL CLEARLY DISCRIMINATES BETWEEN the two spiritual concepts involved in the New Birth, the one pre-natal and the other parturition (birth itself). *Gennao* is used when the whole process of generation covering the internal and external aspects of the subject is the primary consideration, and hence including both male and female means and apparatus of begettal or generation. As stated in *The Companion Bible* [published by the Oxford University Press (see Textual Notes on "begat" to Matthew 1:2-16)]: "When used of the father, *gennao*=to beget or engender; and when used of the mother it means 'to bring forth into the world': but it has not the intermediate sense, 'to conceive' . . . In Matthew 1:1, the noun *genesis* means 'birth'."

Further on Luke 1:57, where "Elizabeth's full time came that she should be delivered, and she brought forth a son," the same authority adds: "Gr. *gennao*. Correctly rendered here, of the mother. Used of the father it='beget'."

2. "Gennao," "Titko," and "Prototokos"

The translation given *gennao* in the A.V. (corrected however both in R.V. and C.V.) is faulty and misleading, giving "born" where only "begotten" should be rendered, and vice versa. The following notes the important passages requiring exact discrimination: John 1:13; 3:1-12; I John 2:29; 3:9; 4:7; 5:1, 18. In every case the thought expressed is "begotten" (the act of generation specially as concerned with the father, the active partner who alone does the begetting and without whom initially conception or the resultant begettal in the mother cannot otherwise take place) rather than "born," namely "to bring forth externally" as concerned with the mother, the passive partner.

The word *titko* is instanced in the following passages, being given in the A.V. the translation shown: (Born) Matthew 2:2; Luke 2:11; Revelation 12:4; (Bring Forth) Matthew 1:21, 23, 25; Luke 1:31; 2:6, 7; Hebrews 6:7; James 1:15; Revelation 12:5, 13.

From the above (noting especially Luke 2:6, 7), it is seen that the child is liberated *only at the birth,* at which time the mother is delivered.

The word *prototokos* (with the prefix *proton,* first) meaning "firstborn," expresses the end result of the begettal, being given a unique biblical significance in relation to our Saviour's resurrection identity. Following are the scriptural occurrences of *prototokos,* with the two instances of faulty translation included where "first-begotten" apears in A.V.: Matthew 1:25; Luke 2:7; Romans 8:29; Colossians 1:15, 18; Hebrews 11:28; 12:23; (in A.V. "first-begotten") Hebrews 1:6; Revelation 1:5.

3.   *The Firstborn from the Dead*

If we note the above references with any appreciable degree of spiritual insight, we shall be able at once to discern that it was not until *after* His Resurrection from the grave on the Sabbath (namely, the seventh day, or otherwise, under its pagan designation, Saturday)[1] which ended the Passover festival A.D. 31, that Jesus became "the first*born*

---

[1] For collateral reading covering this point, see the writer's monograph *The Harmony of the Resurrection* wherein is established Wednesday as the day of the Crucifixion and Saturday as the day of the Resurrection. And for additional illumination, see also Appendix 156, "Six Days Before the Passover," in *The Companion Bible.*

from the dead."—Colossians 1:18; Revelation 1:5; cf. Matthew 28:1, R.V. Scripture is careful to emphasize that the status of the Son all during His entire earthly career and ministry prior to His death and ensuing Resurrection [after "three days and three nights in the heart of the earth," which took Him to the (as then located) underworld Paradise of the Garden of Eden, scripturally called "the third heaven"] was solely that of "the *Only Begotten* of the Father" (Gr. *monogenes*). (See in this connection Matthew 12:40; Luke 23:43; II Corinthians 12:1-4; and note I Corinthians 2:13; Ezekiel 31; Isaiah 14:4-27; Daniel 10:4-6.)

The following texts cover this point: John 1:14, 18; 3:16, 18; Hebrews 11:17; I John 4:9.

Quoting from Psalm 2:7, Paul uses *gennao* to describe the raising of Jesus from the dead in terms of His being "begotten" by the Father. Beckoning to the "men of Israel" at Antioch, Paul declared to them (Acts 13:32-34) the "glad tidings, how that the promise which was made unto the fathers, God hath fulfilled the same unto us their children, in that He hath raised up Jesus again; as it is also written in the second psalm, *Thou art My Son, this day have I BEGOTTEN Thee!* And as concerning that He raised Him up from the dead, now no more to return to corruption, He said on this wise, I will give you the sure mercies of David."

For Him who saw no corruption, He is therefore "begotten" from the Godly view. However, for those who must experience corruption, He becomes "the Firstborn from the dead" from the human view. Each successive avatar or manifestation of Himself, which was threefold, becomes His begettal: namely, 1) when He came forth out of "the bosom of the Father," at the creation, to become the Jehovah or LORD (*Yahweh*) of the Old Testament; 2) when He humbled Himself to descend into a body of flesh to become "JESUS of Nazareth" (*Yahshuah*); 3) when being glorified He next returns to the bosom of the Father to become "the CHRIST of God" (the Messiah or Anointed One, namely, the *Paraclete*). In this sense of the application of "begotten," there is no conflict between *gennao* and *monogenes*.

The Son of God was therefore not "firstborn" until He had passed over via death's portal and poured out His blood, which had hitherto identified Him with the Adamic or human race, namely, the *blood* race of flesh and bones. He inherited His more gloriously fashioned resurrection body *minus all blood,* and acquired in the process His new status as the Second Adam, by which He exactly becomes "a quickening Spirit" and as such the progenitor of *a new creation* (via the Divine Begettal), minus every vestige of the old Adamic characteristics and nature, with its old blood and flesh and bones. In terms of the language in II Corinthians 5:17, this must all pass away, and further, in terms of Tennyson's "wild bells," "rings out the old and rings in the new" divine order.

It is by this means, through the inflow (or intromission) of the Spirit's "Water," that the Second Adam as quickening Spirit achieves the power of the New Begettal whereby the implanting of the seed of His word and faith in His name is accomplished, which in John 3:1-12 is spoken of as being "begotten again." (Cf. also John 7:38, 39; Ephesians 5:26; I Peter 1:3, 23; John 1:12, 13; James 1:18.)

It is thus we read:

> *Romans 8:29:* "For whom He did foreknow [comprehending the New Creation to be *begotten again*], He also did predestinate to be conformed [minus as with Him the old Adamic nature including particularly its blood content] to the image of His Son, that He might be *the Firstborn* among many brethren."

> *Colossians 1:15:* "Who is the image of the invisible God, *the Firstborn* of every creature."

> *Colossians 1:18:* "And He is the Head of the Body, the Church [elsewise, the invisible celestial *ekklesia*]: who is the Beginning, *the Firstborn from the dead,* that in all things He might have the pre-eminence."

Revelation 1:5: "And from Jesus Christ, who is the faithful witness, and *the Firstborn from the dead,* and the Prince of the kings of the earth [namely, KING OF KINGS AND LORD OF LORDS]. Unto Him that loved us, and washed us from our sins in His own blood [which, of course, He completely emptied and spilled, thereby losing every vestige and whit of the old Adamic nature and identity] . . ."

4. The Church of the Firstborn

In the light of the foregoing, we have the key to the exegesis of Hebrews 12:22, 23 which (being addressed to the Hebrews as a nation, the whole twelve tribes of which constituted the Dispersion)[2] reads as follows:

v. 22: "But ye [the Hebrew nation and peoples under the Old Testament covenant applicable to them] are come unto Mount Zion, and unto the City of the Living God, the Heavenly Jerusalem, and to an innumerable company of angels.

v. 23: "To the General Assembly and *Church of the Firstborn* [an expression peculiarly comprehending CHRIST THE FIRSTBORN together with the associated First-fruits pegged to His own resurrection, otherwise *Christ the First-fruits!*],which are written in heaven, and to God the Judge of all, and to the spirits of just [justified] men made perfect."

In other words, as applied to the Hebrew peoples, the season was now rapidly approaching and was even upon them, which would culminate in the Apostolic Generation (the Kingdom of the *Heavens*—Gr. plural—being at hand, as proclaimed in Matthew 10:7 and Luke 10:9), when the

---

[2] The epistle to the Hebrews from the Apostle Paul, as referred to in II Peter 3:1, 15, 16, unquestionably was directed to both the Palestinian Jews and those of the *Diaspora* ("the dispersed among the Gentiles"). See I Peter 1:1; James 1:1; John 7:35 and pertinent Structural Notes in *The Companion Bible.*

spirits of just men, being regenerated and vivified, would be made perfect through acquiring and inheriting their celestial-type bodies, necessary to make them complete and whole and hence *perfect* as celestial beings—that being the thought implicit in this verse.

The above reflects precisely the scene on Mount Zion—Jerusalem above—presented to our view in Revelation 14:1-4 and to be dated A.D. 70, which together with parallel Scriptures further calls our attention to "Christ the First-fruits" as mentioned in I Corinthians 15:23 and collaterally identified with the meaning of the Feast of Pentecost in A.D. 31. In this connection, the types and antitypes pertaining to this occurrence are fully discussed and elaborated in other monograph studies.[3]

The twelve Hebrew tribes as an ethnic whole were even then approaching the divine timetable set forth in their own Old Testament prophecies, when those of the "out-resurrection" would be acquiring and inheriting their celestial-type bodies (or mansions from the Father's house as is comprehended from the meaning of "the spirits of *justified men made perfect*") as the result of their rousing from the graves of earth and their vivification as celestial beings. (Cf. Daniel 9:24-27; 12:1-4, 12, 13; Ezekiel 37; Revelation 12:1-5; 7:1-9. See further John 14:1-4 and II Corinthians 5:1-4.) Without bodies to correspond and thus to complement, these being necessary to overclothe the nucleus or naked germ—the *gumnon-kokkon* in I Corinthians 15:36, 37—represented in their regenerated spirits (both components, spirits and bodies from heaven, being an entirely *new creation* and both representing an acquisition or inheritance that is entirely the gift of God), they could never be said to be perfect.

Hence, in acquiring such bodies, the quota of "out-resurrected" ones from the twelve Hebrew tribes of the Dispersion who were directly affected is here presented as "the General Assembly" of saints, which then becomes nar-

---

[3] See pages 137 and 142.

rowed down to a further distinctive group pinpointed as the out-resurrected *"Ekklesia* of the Firstborn"—namely, the indivisible aggregation of Firstfruits consisting of the Lamb Himself, plus the two complements divinely pegged in the Levitical types to the first and fiftieth days and fulfilling the antitypes connected with the Feast of Pentecost, A.D. 31.

As such, therefore, in a highly definitive sense, the Firstfruits of His Resurrection expressly belong to the apostolic period (A.D. 31 to 70). They who were with Christ in the same historical era were likewise "firstborn from the dead," the only significant difference in this connection being that He, of course, had to be "first"—"that in all things He might have the pre-eminence."

Also, from the additional fact that these Hebrew Firstfruits then living in the apostolic generation were "to be conformed to the image [or exact type] of Him who would be the Firstborn among many brethren," it stands to reason that this conformation pertained to their own similar glorified resurrection, and consequently to their existence as immortal beings in the hereafter following the "birth" of death; and hence to their appearance on the celestial Mount Zion, the Heavenly City Jerusalem, and the seat of God's throne. They were thus to be members, particularly constituting its very Headship, of the celestial Body of Christ, from the clear fact that He was already "the Firstborn from the dead" and they would likewise be conformed into that exact image. Thus, being also "born" or raised from the dead, these Hebrew Firstfruits of the apostolic era were the Elect who would "follow the Lamb withersoever He goeth."

Moreover, in that significant historical time, it was for these Hebrew Firstfruits "the Church of the Firstborn," in its exact literal application and fulfillment. However, for those members subsequently (after the apostolic period) arriving into the glorious heritage of that Body and hence to be included into its celestial composition, it does not signify that as additions they are likewise to be accounted "firstborn." They are identified as a part of the same Body,

but are not its "foundation stones." They, as do the Firstfruits, belong and are part of the living celestial Church of
Jesus Christ the risen, ascended, and glorified Lord!

5. The Feast of Pentecost, A.D. 31

As previously presented in certain monographs which
discuss the subject more fully, and to which attention has
already been called in our preceding topic, the 144,000 Hebrews whom we find spotlighted in Revelation 14:1-4 and
tribally enumerated in Revelation 7:1-8, are the group thus
initially identified as meeting the complete specifications
called for in Hebrews 12:22, 23. This group of Hebrew
saints out of the twelve tribes is now seen in a General Assembly on Mount Zion, the City of the Great King which is
the Heavenly Jerusalem, with the Lamb who is "the Firstborn from the dead," and "the Firstborn among many brethren." We find this group of Hebrew Christians congregated
with the Lamb and the four Zoa and twenty-four Presbyters. The gathering is augmented with the presence, as we
are told in Revelation 5:6-11, of "many angels round about
the throne and the zoa and the presbyters, the number of
whom was ten thousand times ten thousand, and thousands
of thousands," which is exactly *innumerable* to comport
with the language of Hebrews 12:22 and hence exactly the
"many" alluded to in Matthew 27:53.

Moreover, we find in Hebrews 12:22, 23 that the "innumerable company of angels" presented as a constituent
part of "the General Assembly and Church of the Firstborn"
are stated to be on Mount Zion, seen in the context to be
"the City of the Living God, the Heavenly Jerusalem." In
Revelation 5:11 they are shown gathered "round about the
throne," which again puts the same angels on the same
Mount Zion. Hence, "the General Assembly and Church of
the Firstborn," composed of Hebrew and other Old Testament Firstfruits and spotlighted in Revelation 14:1-4 on
Mount Zion "before the throne" are in the same celestial
locale which Matthew 5:34, 35 identifies as being "Jerusa-

lem, the City of the Great King . . . for it is where God's throne is."

From the foregoing, we are able to perceive the identity of the four Zoa and twenty-four Presbyters, together with the 144,000 apostolically dated Hebrews. These, together with the Lamb, are mentioned by the Apostle Paul as "Christ the Firstfruits," being viewed by him as one indivisible whole, as, in fact, Revelation 14:1-4 represents them. These comprise the two complementary categories or allotments seen to be divinely pegged to the double high days—the first and fiftieth—of the *Feast of Pentecost,* A.D. 31, thus fulfilling Matthew 27:50-53; Ephesians 4:8; 1:13, 14; 4:30; Acts 2: 1-4; II Corinthians 1:22 and Revelation 7:3, 4; 14:1-4. See also I Corinthians 15:23.

6. *Christ the Firstfruits*

The first complementary category, divinely pegged to the first day of this double-pronged feast in this memorable year, in keeping with the applicable Levitical types in Leviticus 23:9-22; Deuteronomy 16:9, 10 and Exodus 34:22, was exactly the "multitude (or body) of captives" pointed out in marginal reading to Ephesians 4:8 in the A.V. This band was led captive by Jesus Himself on this first Easter Sunday[4] when He ascended on high, and accepted by the Father as "a sweet savour"—namely, "the sheaf of the wave offering." As recorded by Matthew, we find that "the graves being opend, many bodies of the saints which slept arose and came out of the graves [note!] *after His Resurrection* [which occurred late on the weekly Sabbath, this being *Saturday,*

---

[4] For the benefit of any who may perhaps demur at the use of the terms "Easter" and "Sunday" and such related expressions as pagan in origin and unscriptural, in connection with the present study, we are merely attempting to bring certain spiritual concepts and principles down to the level of common usage where the grapple between truth and error always takes place and the victory of truth over error is of course won. Let this be borne in mind wherever such terms are found.

as seen in Matthew 28:1, R.V.], and went into the Holy
City [namely, Jerusalem above, also called Mount Zion], and
appeared unto many [the innumerable throng of angels]."

This section of the Firstborn—comprising the initial wave
sheaf of the Resurrection Firstfruits—was thus the antitype
of the wave sheaf offering in the harvest festival brought to
light in Leviticus 23:9, 10 and which, by divine ordering,
fell in A.D. 31 on the first Sunday following the Crucifixion.
Perpetuated and since celebrated in Christian tradition as
Easter Sunday, it is therefore a memorable and ineradicable
landmark in the history of the *celestial* Church of Christ—
namely, the living and glorified Body of Christ! The occurrences of this feast in the New Testament being in each
case faultily translated "the first day of the week," when, in
fact, it should be translated as "the first day of the Feast of
Pentecost" (always, however, a Sunday), are as follows:
Matthew 28:1; Mark 16:2; John 20:1, 19; Acts 20:7, 16 and
I Corinthians 16:2, 8.

The correct rendering in these passages should be "the
first (day) of the Sabbaths" (plural). The basic Greek in
this connection (*Te mia ton Sabbaton*), although having specific variations to denote the particular approach of the occasion, is, however, distinctly and divinely intended to
identify this feast and hence to alert us to its onset, and to
the further fact that in scriptural terms we are dealing with
"the first (day) of the (Seven) Sabbaths." Accordingly, the
underlying Greek signifies the beginning of the Feast of
Weeks or, even more specifically, the Feast of the Harvest
Firstfruits, otherwise the Feast of Pentecost (from the Greek
pentekostos, meaning fiftieth day, or by extension of meaning fifty days). In terms of the number of whole weeks involved (cf. Leviticus 23:15, 16 and Deuteronomy 16:9), the
Feast of the Seven Sabbaths gives the exact count and duration period for this particular festival.

The word "day" (not in the original) is rightly supplied,
as *mia* is feminine, and so must agree with a feminine noun
understood (this being *hemera* for day), while *sabbaton* in

the plural is neuter. The expression according to *The Companion Bible* (see Textual Note on John 20:1) is not a Hebraism, and "sabbaths" should therefore not be rendered "week" (sing.) as in the A.V. and the R.V. This Easter Sunday, being the day which *followed* our Lord's Resurrection, consequently was "the first day" (which was always a Sunday, being the day after the weekly Sabbath) of the fifty days for reckoning the "Seven Sabbaths" or "Seven Weeks" to the closing of Pentecost, it, too, always falling on a Sunday.

In fulfilling the types which pointed out the wave sheaf offering of the first day, as presented in the resurrection and ascension to glory of the four Zoa and twenty-four Presbyters who were thus bracketed as beginning Firstfruits (which divinely fitted them into the category of the Firstborn) to be credited to the Old Testament dispensation, our Antitype had by His own death and resurrection come into possession of "the keys of Death and Hell" (in the Gr. *Thanatos* and *Hades*). "For this purpose the Son of God was manifested, that He might destroy the works of the Devil," thereby completely to eradicate and "destroy him that had the power of death."—Revelation 1:18; I John 3:8; Hebrews 2:14; and Matthew 16:18.

The second complementary category of Firstfruits belonging to the same contemporary harvest and covering the *two wave loaves* in the types, becomes similarly pegged to the fiftieth day of the same Pentecostal Feast in the same year (A.D. 31), through the token device or arrangement of the *Divine Sealing* as constructively manifested in the outpouring of *THE Holy Spirit* (Gr. with the article *to Pneuma to Hagion*) on the fullness of the Day of Pentecost itself. Thus, being foreknown and predestined (according to Romans 8:29, 30), the 144,000 were divinely numbered and accounted for in advance, forty years ahead of the date of their actual redemption and ascension to glory *circa* A.D. 70, when the occasion of the Great Tribulation (otherwise Zion's travailing) arrived.

However, from the Levitical types which give us our correct bearings, the divine dating of this redemption in connection with the second phasing of the Resurrection or Harvest Firstfruits correctly belongs to A.D. 31. The fulfillment of the types covering the complementary Firstfruits in their entirety, broken down to their two respective Pentecostal phases, accordingly becomes pegged to both the first and fiftieth days of the Feast of Pentecost as occurring in that memorable year of Divine Grace and super-abounding love and goodwill to the whole of mankind.—Ephesians 3:1-9.

The Feast of Pentecost is what now gives us the correct measure and estimate of a unique divine enterprise which in its duration—beginning A.D. 31—is to last into the eons, or ages, and which in its extent and range, together with its over-all coverage and dimensions, is therefore eonian. It also gives us the correct picture of an inseparable celestial partnership which links together into one indivisible whole those divinely sealed on the Day of Pentecost itself with those who earlier, and quite unspectacularly, came out of their graves on that glorious Easter morn nearly 2000 years ago —the day which followed the Son's own unspectacular Resurrection at the Sabbath evening's dusk. The Feast of Pentecost, being indivisible, even though separated between its Levitical confines by an interval of fifty days, is hence what really gives us the vital perspective and true focus (including its eonian wrap-up) of "Christ the Firstfruits!"

7. The "Birth" of the Hebrew Manchild

The key to the New Birth further unlocks the mystery and emphasizes the meaning of the Manchild "born" to the symbolic Woman of Revelation 12:1-5. "The Woman clothed with the sun, and the moon under her feet, and upon her head a crown of twelve stars," is stated to be "a great sign" (from the Gr. semeion) and not "a great wonder" as it appears in the A.V. The symbolism is exactly de-

scriptive, or explanatory, of the dream recorded in Genesis
37:9 which Joseph had in Egypt, wherein he narrates "the
sun and the moon and the eleven stars made obeisance to
me," he being the twelfth star which completes this wreath.
The context of this language clearly shows its application in
symbolic terms to the embryonic nation of Israel as subsequently evolving into the twelve ethnic tribes of Israel.
(See Appendix 12, "The Stars Also," in *The Companion
Bible,* which discusses the twelve signs of the Zodiac and
the divine symbolism therein expressed.)

The Heavenly Woman in Revelation 12:4 is thus a definitive symbol of the Hebrew people under the Old Testament in a pending state of resurrection and ascension, being
representative of the fortunes and recompense of the twelve
tribes in the Judgment. This itself is coincident with the
close of the Scriptural Age and the arrival of the Messianic
Kingdom, the Kingdom of the Heavens (Gr. pl.), as divinely
envisaged in the New Testament.—Matthew 13:39, 40; 24:3;
10:7, 23 and Luke 10:9-14. Hence, as interpreted by Isaiah
66:7-10, the Manchild is of direct Hebrew descent, com-
plexion, origin, and identification, and accordingly the
Woman herself is of an all-Hebrew composition and cast, in
keeping with the comparable specifications for the Manchild.
As written in this latter Scripture, we read:

"7) Before she travailed, she brought forth; before her
pain came, she was delivered of a manchild. 8)Who hath
heard such a thing? who hath seen such things? Shall the
earth be made to bring forth in one day? *or shall a nation
be born at once?* for as soon as Zion travailed, she *brought
forth* her children. 9) *Shall I bring to the birth, and not
cause to bring forth? saith the* LORD: shall I cause to bring
forth, and shut the womb? saith thy God. 10) Rejoice ye
with Jerusalem, and be glad with her, all ye that love her:
rejoice for joy with her, all ye that mourn for her."

Plainly, in the foregoing reference, we have the unfolding of the birth to the Celestial Woman of Revelation 12
of not only one but *two important Manchildren* (apart from

her subsequent "remnant seed," also alluded to in the Isaiah quote) comprehending the Levitical Firstfruits in the two corresponding segments of the Feast of Pentecost as we have scanned these already, to which this Old Testament passage literally applies. Namely (1), the four Zoa and twenty-four Presbyters who were "born," as verse 7 here tells us, "*before* the Woman travailed, when she brought forth and was delivered of a Manchild [being the *first* Manchild] *before her pain came.*" This refers to those resurrected, as Matthew 27: 50-53 significantly discloses, to receive the inheritance of their redemption bodies and thus be "made perfect."

Hence, in Isaiah 66:7 we have our attention directly called to the events occurring on the first day of the Feast of Pentecost, A.D. 31, forty years before the Great Tribulation—synonymous with the pain of travailing in childbirth, which Romans 8:19-23 likewise clearly reflects. The Great Tribulation came upon the Hebrew people in the land of Judea (A.D. 70), at which time their Levitical complement was "born as soon as Zion travailed"! And thus we have (2), the 144,000 representing the *second* Manchild (this being the Hebrew Manchild) who were "delivered" to the same Celestial Woman at a different time, being as we are told all "*born at once*" and so all together "in one day." "For as soon as Zion travailed, she brought forth her children," which is to say, she brought forth *again,* or the *second* time! The second Manchild thus delivered, representing the last of the Pentecostal Firstfruits, was also the curtain-raiser and the immediate prelude for the complete harvest reaping which followed in only a matter of days in the divine reckoning of time.

Accordingly, being "born" in scriptural terminology comprehends and expresses the language of redemption and salvation in terms of spiritual biology, when we inherit, acquire, and come into actual literal possession of our celestial-type habitations from heavens, *being the free gift of God,* provided through the Son!—II Corinthians 5:2 with which cp. John 14:2 and I Corinthians 15:37, 38.

8. The "Exanastasis" or "Out-Resurrection" in Philippians 3:11

The Manchild in Revelation 12:1-5, being the second of the two manchildren of Isaiah 66:7-10, thus proves to be the 144,000 "out-resurrected" Hebrew saints, identified with the *exanastasis* of Philippians 3:11, who were redeemed from the earth. They, being "born all at once and in one day" and sealed out of the twelve tribes of ethnic (or literal) Israel with the "Holy Spirit of promise," thereby received the divine pledge (the token down payment which should guarantee its execution and fulfillment) of their redemption in the Apostolic Generation. This is clearly seen in the manifestation and outpouring of the Holy Spirit in A.D. 31 on the Day of Pentecost, the complete realization of which came forty years later in A.D. 70 "as soon as Zion travailed."

In this connection, the Apostle Paul in Romans 8:18-23 relates the absolute timing and application of Zion's travailing to the Apostolic Generation of which he himself was a present and living participant. In keeping with his own personal anticipations in the matter, he was a beneficiary of no mean distinction, being (as he has apprised us in Phillippians 3:5-11) "of the stock of Israel, of the tribe of Benjamin, *an Hebrew of the Hebrews*": all of which "he counted loss for Christ," adding, "and do count them but dung, that I may win Christ . . . that I may know Him and the power of His Resurrection [here simply the *anastasis*], and the fellowship of His sufferings, being made conformable unto His death, if by any means I might attain unto the *out-resurrection from the dead* [in the Greek, and its only occurrence, the *exanastasis*, signifying his definite desire and his unquenchable hope to attain his *birth* from the dead in that very generation]."

In other words, Paul was emphatically announcing his willingness and his determination to forfeit, sacrifice, and renounce all his natural rights under the old ritual law, even including those to which as a Hebrew descendant he was divinely entitled under the Old Covenant of works, for the

greater heritage and glory under grace and the certainty
of his prospects as a celestial which as a Hebrew Christian
he would now have through faith in the risen Living Christ
"and *the power of His Resurrection.*"

Paul was even more keenly conscious that being a Hebrew Christian in itself was not enough to enable him to
make the divine grade. As he well realized, he would have
to meet the exacting divine specifications laid down in Revelation 14:4, 5, which required that every one of the 144,000
qualifying "Firstfruits" of this particular Pentecostal category must also be celibates. It was said of them in addition,
"And in their mouth was found no guile, for they are without fault before the throne of God."

As the Apostle took pains to point out in I Corinthians
7:25-33, he had nothing personal against the institution of
marriage per se, contending in Hebrews 13:4 that "marriage
is honorable in all, and the bed undefiled." He therefore
had no laws or rules to lay down, even pausing to announce
that he "had no commandment of the Lord," but was simply
outlining his own personal judgment and opinion. In other
words, he was not attempting to be dogmatic or legalistic
about the matter. He averred (I Corinthians 7:6, 7) he was
"speaking this by permission and not of commandment";
adding, "For I would that all men were even as I myself":
but said further that it was a matter for each one's own personal decision and outlook, depending on the "proper gift
of God, one after this manner and another after that."

It was only for himself that he was setting his sights
supremely high. In this respect, it was purely a matter of
voluntary choice on his part for the glory and honor en-
visioned and for the greater rewards and blessings he was
sure would follow. For him it was not merely a question of
salvation; he knew he had that through divine grace, which
of course he did not have to earn. It was now a question of
the extension of salvation, the divine rewards he had to earn
for himself and for which, in its farthest application and
meaning, each saved Christian must earn for himself.

The Apostle consequently made the necessary sacrifice and so went all out to qualify himself as a "virgin"—this being an unmarried priest or prophet or saint of God, under the strictest voluntary sacred vows never to be "defiled with women." All of this was in line with his carefully uttered, inspired testimony, in which he said that he was ready to "count all things but loss for the excellency of the knowledge of Christ Jesus my Lord: for whom I have suffered the loss of all things, and do count them but dung, *that I may win Christ.*"—Philippians 3:5-11.

Paul the Apostle was hopeful, although at the moment he did not realize it absolutely, that he too had been "sealed with the Holy Spirit of promise, which was to be the earnest [in terms of the divine down payment] of his inheritance until the redemption [or birth] of the purchased possession." Hence he expressed his earnest concern, his intense preoccupation, and his zealous striving to attain the "out-resurrection" as one to be labeled a Firstfruit in the special group to which he definitely belonged by virtue of his own *sealing*; namely, with the second increment bracketed in the types to the Day of Pentecost itself, as this was fulfilled in A.D. 31. And to this end he therefore states: "I press toward the mark for the prize of the high calling of God in Christ Jesus." —Philippians 3:14.

Moreover, we find the same exact Hebrew specifications presented in connection with the *exanastasis* of Philippians 3:11 as are called for in the requirements for the Divine Sealing, presented under the Levitical types previously noted and also from a consideration of the twelve-tribed Manchild in Revelation 12:1-5; 7:4-8 and 14:1-4. Paul quite significantly presents the question of his "out-resurrection" as it pertains to himself personally and to his own individual prospects and qualifications in terms of his own ethnic origin and descent, together with his tribal identity. To be a *Hebrew* by ethnic descent was, above all, a definite "must" which all participants and inheritors in the sealing had to meet in that generation, and Paul was particularly conscious of this divine requirement. As proof, he went to extreme but quite understandable pains to document his ethnic identity and background, as he does in both Philippians 3:5 and Romans 11:1.

The Apostle thus made much of the important fact that he was "of the stock of Israel, of the tribe of Benjamin, *an Hebrew of the Hebrews.*" And that was the clincher which proved his eligibility for such exclusive company—this being the 144,000 and hence "Christ the Firstfruits." The question of tribal pedigree was the *sine qua non,* the indispensable requirement, for the divine passport necessary to any redemption as "Firstfruits," for those who were to be classified as "firstborn." Being linked by divine right to the identity of the Hebrew Manchild, we are not at all surprised that such tribal pedigree, with its emphasis on ethnic origin and descent, is firmly tied to the *exanastasis* which Paul, in terms of the highest emotion, fervently and passionately talks about in Philippians 3:11.

9. *Zion's Travailing*

The significance and application to the Apostolic Generation of Romans 8:18-23 should now be plain. It is narrated by Paul as follows:

"18) For I reckon that the sufferings of *this present time* [in the Apostolic Generation] are not worthy to be compared with the glory which shall be revealed *in us* [namely, the firstfruits themselves—in those of that generation including the Apostle himself who accordingly had all received the sealing as Firstfruits]. 19) For the earnest expectation of the creature waiteth for *the manifestation of the sons of God.* 20) For the creature was made subject to vanity, not willingly, but by reason of Him who hath subjected the same in hope, 21) because the creature itself also shall be delivered from the bondage of corruption [which death in the old Adam entails but which, in terms of spiritual biology, equates to birth—the New Birth!] unto the glorious

liberty of the children [sons] of God. 22) For we know that
the whole creation groaneth and travaileth in pain together
until *now* [again calling attention to the apostolic generation
in which this was happening, with all the divine omens
pointing to the swift approach and imminent onset of the
Great Tribulation culminating in the events of A.D. 70].
23) And not only they, *but ourselves also* [in and of and
belonging to that generation!] *which have the Firstfruits of
the Spirit* [attesting the sealing which put the Father's Name
upon them, with its aura of exclusive possession: intended
to give divine assurance to them in advance, in the earnest
and pledge thus received as firstfruits of their celestial in-
heritance], even we ourselves groan within ourselves, waiting for the adoption, *to wit, the redemption of our body."*
(For parallel consideration, see James 1:18; also John 5:
24-29 and Daniel 12:1, 2 and Ezekiel 37.)

Thus, in terms of travailing which is the language of
pregnancy and childbirth as used in the field of spiritual
biology (and sometimes also referred to under the heading
of *phallic symbolism,* to which the whole subject of the
New Birth is in fact related), we have the true significance,
application, and timing of the *Birth of the Hebrew Manchild* (the *second* of the two manchildren born to the Heavenly Woman, and the one focussed in Revelation 12:1-5)
in the interpretive wording of the Apostle Paul himself. It
is further reflected, as has been stated, in the *exanastasis* of
Philippians 3:11, which expresses the delivery of "birth"
from the dead along with the simultaneous fruition of redemption bodies derived from heaven. Zion's travailing,
therefore, becomes correctly dated *circa* A.D. 70, as seen
from Matthew 23:36 through 24:1-35.

10.   John 5:24-29 Spotlights the Two Manchildren

With reference to the two manchildren as brought to
light in Isaiah 66:7-10, the Saviour Himself in John 5:29
furnishes the most conclusive and authoritative evidence
concerning the twin nature of their Pentecostal identity, to-

gether with the imminence and inevitable certitude of their resurrection arrival, or "birth," as this pertained to the very year of His discourse.

Concerning the first Manchild (pegged to the first day of the Feast of Pentecost A.D. 31 and comprising the "birth" of the four Zoa and twenty-four Presbyters), we read: "Verily, verily, I say unto you, The hour is coming, *and now is* [therefore A.D. 31], when the dead shall hear the voice of the Son of God: and they that hear shall live." In Matthew 27:50-53 we have the documented fulfillment of this positive utterance in the following record: "Jesus, when He had cried with *a loud voice,* yielded up the ghost. And, behold, the veil of the temple was rent in twain from the top to the bottom; and the earth did quake, and the rocks rent; and the graves were opened; and many of the bodies of the saints which slept arose, and came out of the graves *after His Resurrection,* and went into *the Holy City* [Jerusalem above] and appeared unto many." These—the initial increment of His own Resurrection or Pentecostal Firstfruits—had heard His voice, and so hearing they lived, as He had declared would be the case.

The second Manchild is pegged to the Day of Pentecost itself and comprises the "birth" of the 144,000, itself referring to the year A.D. 31 through the token arrangement of the *sealing.* This divinely anticipates their birth—not actually concluded until forty years later—that was itself to be the curtain raiser and prelude to the ensuing general harvest reaping to follow swiftly thereafter. As therefore related to all Israel under the Old Testament economy of law and works we next read: "Marvel not at this: for the hour is coming [hence A.D. 70], in the which ALL that are in the graves shall hear His voice, and shall come forth; they that have done good unto the resurrection of life, and they that have done evil unto the resurrection of damnation."—John 5:28, 29. How exactly, now, do we find these words comporting with Daniel 12:1-3, which reads: "And many of them that sleep in the dust of the earth shall awake, some to eonian life, and some to shame and eonian contempt!" As shown in the context of this Old Testament passage, Daniel was himself assured that although "he should rest, he would stand in his lot at the end of the 1335 days," thus tying the prophetic events envisaged in this chapter to the time when both "the City and the Sanctuary would be destroyed," namely, A.D. 70!—Daniel 9:26.

Being dispatched to strengthen and enlighten him with heavenly wisdom concerning the special events divinely bracketed to the period of the Crucifixion and the Destruction of Jerusalem, the angel Gabriel gave specific reassurance to the prophet Daniel that those events would be *"noted in the Scripture of truth!"* In other words, Daniel was thereby being put on notice, although centuries ahead of their occurrence, that the events of John 5:24-29 (involving the two Manchildren) were certain of exact fulfillment in the Apostolic Era, being of a nature so extraordinary and profound, so significant and exceptional, and so outstanding and certain in the realm of Gospel truth as to be the most notable, the most memorable, the most celebrated, and the most sublime in all the annals of sacred history.

The angel Gabriel had thus been commissioned to put the explicit divine imprimatur upon A.D. 31 and A.D. 70 as representing the respective resurrection dates of the Two Manchildren comprising the Pentecostal Firstfruits that were pegged to the two horns of this Feast, along with the completed harvest resurrection embracing all Israel as related to the Old Testament economy which covenanted this final result. (See Daniel 10:18-21; 12:1-3; 9:20-27.) In this connection, the twice-uttered *"Verily, verily!"* of John 5:25 itself redoubles the same emphasis and the same positive guarantee of fulfillment that the angel Gabriel puts upon the same resurrection events spanning A.D. 31 to 70. It was as though Jesus was instead confirming to His disciples: *"So noteworthy and true, so inevitable the certitude, so unforgettable the transaction, so infallible and unique, and indeed so ineradicable and certain for all time to come, will the ful-*

*fillment of all these things be in this your very own genera-
tion!"*

Moreover, from Ezekiel 37, we glean further the exact
nature and type of resurrection harvest envisaged for Old
Testament Israel, described as the "coming together of
bones, bone to its bone, the sinews and flesh laid over these,
with the skin covering them from above," the whole knit together and animated with the Spirit or breath of life. Even
as the first Manchild was raised in this manner, yet unseen
and unknown to those who were keeping watch, the Romans
as well as the unbelieving Jews; even so also is the subsequent "birth" of the second Manchild and of all those associated with the general resurrection harvest of this significant period, still unperceived by many who refuse to accept
or believe the Word of God. The foregoing multiple "births"
which, up to that period, account for all of Zion's children
"in the regeneration when the Son of Man should be sitting
in the throne of His glory" are at once notable and interesting, in that they were *visual* only to those "in the Spirit"—
all others being purblind, having eyes but seeing not. In
their fulfillment, there was of course nothing theatrical or
spectacular about these matters to bring them to the attention of any except those who were divinely nurtured, indoc-
trinated, and oriented in the things of the Spirit. And this,
The New Birth as it progresses thematically attempts to
clarify and focus.

As we have seen, Zion's travailing which produced the
"birth" of her children synchronized with the Destruction
of Jerusalem, which in turn marked the close of the Old
Testament Jewish economy. The year A.D. 70 was thus
God's dividing line which closed one eon or age, and ushered in its successor—the present economy of grace in
which we are now living. This may be difficult for some to
see, or for many to accept. But the writer prefers, nevertheless, to be in line "not in the words which man's wisdom
teacheth, but which the Holy Spirit teacheth."—I Corinthians
2:13. In Topic No. 12 the writer will continue with a further
discussion of "The 'Eons.' "

11. The Four Zoa⁵ and Twenty-four Presbyters

As to the identity of the four Zoa who, in Matthew 27: 50-53, were roused out of their graves to come forth and ascend (along with the twenty-four Presbyters) to Celestial Jerusalem, "the City of the Great King," our attention immediately turns to the remnant of an elohic race—the inhabitants of the earth before the inauguration of the Adamic creation. They are variously described in the opening chapters of the Bible as "the beasts of the field," or "cherubim," "elohim," "the sons of the elohim," and also the "nephilim" or fallen ones. From all pertinent scriptural considerations, they were a pre-Adamic race who, after the downfall of man, were placed for dwelling in a geographical region east of Eden, also termed "the land of Nod," namely, the land of the fugitives, wanderers, vagabonds, or nomads, which served as a buffer zone between the cast-out Adamites and the Tree of Life.—Genesis 3:24; 4:16, and 3:5 and 6:1-4.

As a fallen and corrupt race who shared occupancy of the earth with the struggling infant human race (the Adamites) during the prediluvian era, in an uneven struggle which proved disadvantageous and ruinous to the latter, they were themselves the subjects of divine mercy, compassion, and redeeming grace and the recipients of the covenant plan of salvation which included the Adamites. Hence the account of the unveiling of their concurrent redemption in Revelation 5:9, 10, where (as *seraphim* rather than as cherubim) we find them exulting, as the original Greek reading literally tells us: "And they [the four Zoa and the twenty-four Presbyters] sung a new song, saying, Thou art worthy to take the Book [or Scroll] and to open the seals thereof: for Thou wast slain, and hast redeemed [most Texts omit *us*] to God by Thy blood out of every kindred and tongue and people [referring exactly to the twenty-four Presbyters],

---

⁵ *Zoa* (plural of *zoon*) are animals or beasts, i.e., living creatures. First occurs in Hebrews 13:11. Occurs twenty times. They are distinguished from angels in Revelation 5:8, 11. Elsewhere mentioned in Ezekiel, first and tenth chapters.

and *they* [not we] shall reign on the earth."[6] (See also reading in *Concordant Version,* and for a further insight on the fourfold order of this elohic race, divinely presented as cherubim or beasts of the field, see Appendix 41 in *The Companion Bible.*)

The twenty-four Presbyters are concomitantly discerned from the foregoing as members of the Adamic or *blood* race, in significant contrast to the cherubic orders, being redeemed as they were "out of every kindred and tongue and people and nation." As initial Firstfruits divinely pegged to the wave sheaf offering under the Levitical types of that day, they had to be twenty-four Old Testament worthies among whom would be reckoned such of the patriarchs as Abel and Seth, Noah and Shem, Abraham and Lot, Isaac and Jacob, Moses and Aaron, Joshua and others. And, of course, mention is to be made of Job (1726-1516 B.C.) in connection with this initial classification, because of the firm and emphatic testimony which he gives in anticipation of his own resurrection and the certainty of it. As he states in Job 19:25-27: "For I know that my Redeemer liveth, and that He shall stand *at the latter* [*day*] upon the earth: and though after my skin worms destroy this body, yet in my flesh shall I see God: whom I shall see for myself, and mine eyes shall behold, and not another; though my reins be consumed within me."

"Day" as used in this passage by the translators is a supplied word, which means that it does not appear at all in the original Hebrew. It does, however, call attention to the *latter time of the age* (the eon as divinely delimited and

---

[6] The twenty-four Presbyters, now heavenly beings, in their celestial functioning represent "the pattern" after which David arranged his twenty-four courses of the sons of Aaron, combining for them the offices of prophet, priest, and king, as they speak for God, present the prayers of others, and sit on thrones.—I Chronicles 24:3-5 and cp. Hebrews 8:5 and 9:23. Revelation 4:4, 10 shows the Presbyters with "crowns of gold," the *only other* celestial wearer being the Son Himself (see 14:14 and 19:12). The New Song in Revelation 5:8-10 therefore has relevancy *only to them!*

circumscribed) as this would be bracketed between the Crucifixion and the Destruction of Jerusalem (A.D. 31-70). Matthew 13:39 expressly tells us (in the Greek) that the *Resurrection Harvest* would definitely mark "the end of the *age*," and the context of Matthew 24:3 at once harmonizes this event with the Destruction of Jerusalem in A.D. 70. Daniel 9:24-27, taken with 12:1-3, further confirms the correctness of this harmony.

Accordingly, as next pointed out in Revelation 4:4, 10, 11 and 5:14, Job had the immense satisfaction and joy of at last finding all his cherished hopes fulfilled in the resurrection brought to light in Matthew 27:52, 53, which immediately followed his Redeemer's own triumphant Resurrection from the grave: "that in all things He might have the pre-eminence." And the exact year of Job's resurrection, as it was for the other twenty-three Presbyters, was hence A.D. 31.

In this connection, again note that all of the foregoing took place in the *latter days*—or time—of the period (the eon) which ended in A.D. 70, as divinely authenticated by no less an authority than Jesus Himself in Matthew 13:39, 40 (with which cp. 24:3, 34) where the word translated "world" is the Greek *aion*, transliterated eon, a time-word meaning "age." At this juncture, note further I Corinthians 2:13-16, and then refer to our next topic which touches briefly on the subject of the eons and their scriptural meaning.

As a parenthetical matter, we now take time to notice that both Enoch and Elijah, the two witnesses in Revelation 11:3-12, are also to be listed with this august collection of celestial personages with an earth origin. Their resurrection follows their apocalyptic set-to with the Beast powers in the Judgment (A.D. 70) when they were killed and their dead bodies left lying in the streets of Jerusalem below, i.e., in the land of Palestine. And they ascended heavenward "after three days and a half, when the Spirit of Life from God entered into their dead bodies, and they heard a voice from heaven saying unto them, Come up hither [to their celestial seats around the throne]. And they ascended up to heaven in a cloud." This, of course, was the *first* heaven of God's Throne and Inner Presence, namely, Celestial Jerusalem, the *cloud* consisting of the "innumerable company of angels" and the four Zoa together with their own twenty-two brethren, who escorted them thither.

Thus, prior to this ascent, there were *just twenty-two elders* in the select resurrection group of Matthew 27:52, 53 who preceded from the same earthly locale in Jerusalem—the point of rendezvous with the already risen Lord as He was about to begin His first ascension. The full elected complement at last was present only when the two witnesses (Enoch and Elijah) ascended to their places around the throne. Consequently, Revelation 4:4-11 (where we find them included) is to be dated *for them* A.D. 70, but in turn divinely credited to A.D. 31, the effective date for the group as a whole.

Accordingly, this pinpoints the fact, even as we are to expect in the fulfillment of the Scriptures which cannot lie, that "it is appointed unto men once to die, but after this the judgment," which could be no less true for Enoch and Elijah than for any other human being. *They had to die, too!* (See Genesis 5:23, 24; Hebrews 11:5; II Kings 2:11; Matthrew 17:1-5 and Hebrews 9:27; Romans 5:12 and I Corinthians 15:22.)

As to who may *not* properly be included among the twenty-four elder statesmen, David and Isaiah can safely be eliminated, we believe. In Psalm 17:15 we find the Psalmist exclaiming: "As for me, I will behold Thy face in righteousness: I shall be satisfied, when I awake in Thy likeness." But in spite of this eloquent and confident testimony, we know for sure from Acts 2:29-34 that "the patriarch David" did not ascend into the heavens with the blessed contingent who arose from their graves in A.D. 31. Hence, he may not be numbered among the twenty-four Ancients. And Isaiah is undoubtedly another who, along with Daniel, would stand in his allotment at the end of the 1335 days (which takes us into A.D. 70), because by a further process of elimination he could not reasonably be among the 144,000 who, being *Hebrew Christians* out of the Apostolic Era and themselves the contemporaries of Jesus and therefore among those confessing the Name of Christ, were exclusively selected and sealed for redemption with the Holy Spirit of promise, namely, *Himself!* (Cf. II Corinthians 3:17.) Him also (Isaiah) we find confidently and expectantly proclaiming: "Thy dead men shall live, *together with my dead body shall they arise.*[7] Awake and sing, ye that dwell in the dust: for thy dew is as the dew of herbs, and the earth shall cast out the dead." In the context of his statement, Isaiah was definitely referring to the time of Zion's travailing "in the land of Judah," this being of course A.D. 70. (Cf. Isaiah 26:1, 17-19.)

Are we not justified, therefore, to count Job in with the elder statesmen comprising the initial category of Pentecostal Firstfruits, namely, the four Zoa and twenty-four Presbyters, divinely bracketed to the year A.D. 31?

In this connection, Job throws some further interesting light on the question of his own succession to glory and its timing. Notice that (in Job 14:13-15) he says:

"O that Thou wouldest hide me in the grave [Heb. *sheol*], that Thou wouldest keep me secret, until Thy wrath be past, *that Thou wouldest appoint me a set time, and remember me!* If a man die, shall he live again? all the days of my appointed time will I wait till my change [i.e., any improvement for the better, hence connoting *succession*] come. *Thou wilt call* (!) *and I will answer Thee*: Thou wilt have a desire to the work of Thine hands."

Unquestionably, the answer to Job's prayer and his hopes for the resurrection of the just is centered in John 5:25-27

---

[7] Some authorities (Goodspeed, Moffat, Septuagint, and others) make no mention of "my dead body." *The Companion Bible,* however, does not note this exception.

and Matthew 27:50-53 (further reflected in Revelation 4: 4, 10, 11 and 5:8-10, 14), when in answer to the voice of the dying Saviour on the cross which called him forth, he arose triumphantly out of the tomb—thus to answer the *divine call!* For Job, his "set time" was A.D. 31: and "the days of his appointed time in which he was to wait till his change," or succession, therefore ended with the first day of the Feast of Pentecost in that year, being also under Levitical law the first day of the week; hence *Easter Sunday!* The resurrection call for Job is therefore considerably past, by some nineteen centuries elapsed time.

12. *The Eons in Scripture and Their Meaning*

The subject of the eons is one which we expect to delve into and elaborate in a subsequent Bible study, because of its transcendent importance and its identification with the Gospel proclamation and the divine plan of salvation, which can be perceived from the reading of John 3:16 as follows: "For God so loved the world that He gave His only begotten Son, that whosoever believeth in Him should not perish, but have *age-lasting* life." Which is to say, in more accurate terminology, *eonian* life, divinely used to express life in the duration of the eons. Starting with the eon in which we are all presently living, it is hence the successor to the eon which by divine creation (as in Hebrews 1:2 where "worlds" is in the Greek *aion*) expressly closed in A.D. 70.

Suffice it to say at this juncture, and only by way of introducing the subject, that, as scripturally defined, the eon is a limited portion of time with a beginning and ending, and exactly measurable in terms of the yardstick of "day and night." (See Revelation 20:10.)

As such, therefore, the eons collectively represent a considerable extension of time unfolding, in successive stages and periods, into the indefinite future; that is to say, unfolding into what has been chosen to be otherwise translated "everlasting," "eternity," and "forever" in our ordinary versions. Nevertheless, in the aggregate, even as singly, they have not only a beginning but a very definite ending, *a cut-off or critical point divinely called in Holy Writ the consummation of the eons, or present series of ages; namely,* "THE END!"—I Corinthians 15:24.

Beyond this critical point, a new cycle of ages will, of course, open up, but our only concern at the moment is with salvation as limited and confined to the current cycle; this being, in divine terms, eonian life.

With this scriptural usage in mind, *The Companion Bible* under Appendix 195 discusses "The Different Ages and Dispensations of God's Dealing with Men," in order to focus this timely warning:

> "Nothing but confusion can arise from reading into one dispensation that which relates to another. To connect what God said and did in one dispensation, with another in which His administration was on an altogether different principle, is to ensure error. And finally, to take doctrine of late revelation and read it into the time when it was 'hidden' leads to disaster."

And this is precisely the sort of disaster we are facing in the instances before us (presented in preceding topic) pertaining to Job's redemptive expectation in "the latter days" and the language used by the Divine Teacher Himself. Jesus gives the Holy Spirit's own illumination of the events intended to mark the end of the Old Testament age but which, as always, is foolishness to the theological pundits and the ecclesiastical "princes of this age" (Gr. *aion*), because "the natural man receiveth not the things of the Spirit of God: neither can he know them, because they are spiritually discerned," and are hence known only in terms of "the words which the Holy Spirit teacheth."—I Corinthians 2:4-15; Romans 12:16 and Proverbs 26:12. Alas, due to this fact most present-day prophetic calculations are consequently and inevitably some 2000 years out of the way!

As scripturally defined and spiritually analyzed, the

events which marked the Destruction of Jerusalem in A.D. 70 also brought the Old Testament age to its fateful and harrowing close, and thereby introduced the *suntelia* of the eon. The *suntelia* is the overlapping of the "ends" which, in Matthew 24:3 (as well as in 13:39, 40, 49 and 28:10), tell the story of the meeting point that tied together two distinct ages—one representing the closing "end" and the other the opening "end"—and both meeting the exact time specification by divine ordering.[8]

Thus, as one eon was ending, another was just beginning; as one was drawing to its awesome and tragic close, the other as it opened up was scheduled to bring in *a new order of things*, the two "ends" represented by this juxtaposition of events being "the *suntelia* of the eon," in the specification of Matthew 24:3. The former constituted the definitive landmark which, to the accompaniment of an unprecedented time of trouble with tragic repercussions (unparalleled suffering and misery and indescribable groaning and travailing), attested the fulfillment of the Old Testament Resurrection harvest including its subsidiary Firstfruits, which the Apostle Paul mentions in Romans 8:19-23. The latter was to bring in the succeeding eon; namely, the present era of grace and so-called Gentile administration in which we are now living.

Correct scriptural usage both in the Hebrew and in the Greek expresses the idea of *segments of time* in several different ways, certain words[9] being used to convey important distinctions, but our limited range unfortunately does not permit us to take these up at this time. However, we can point out, as instances from the eonian angle, that

---

[8] Although a different Greek word is used (*telos*), I Corinthians 10:11 uses the expression "the *ends* of the ages" to convey the same idea: the joining point of two ages—the arrival of one to its closing "end," the departure of the other from its opening "end"—and this verse of course has application to the Apostolic Generation.

[9] *chronos, kairos, oikonomia,* etc. See *Companion Bible*, Appendix 195.

we have the "age" singly as well as the "ages" plurally; "the age of the ages" as well as "the ages of the ages"; and "all the generations of the age of the ages"; together with other unique divine differentiations. All of these, in terms of the yardstick of day and night, denote measurable portions of time with both beginnings and endings. In this connection, see further in *Companion Bible*, " 'Everlasting', 'Eternal', 'Forever', Etc.," Appendix 151.

Accordingly, the earnest truth seeker who is also an assiduous Bible student must be careful to follow the mind of God as He has revealed these important matters pertaining to the eons in the Scriptures, that is to say, in the original languages. Especially is this important concerning the question of eonian salvation and eonian life as significantly related to the divine plan of the eons, or ages. Of course the corollary extension of meaning in such terms as eonian judgment, eonian punishment, eonian condemnation and eonian torment is equally important.

The life that is eonian in its duration and extent is the same as the torment (popularly called hellfire—this being purely figurative and symbolic in its exact divine connotation—but in certain ecclesiastical circles called Purgatory) which is also eonian. One is of course the Life abundant, while the other, reserved for "the fearful and unbelieving, the abominable and murderers, whoremongers and sorcerers, idolaters and all liars," is scripturally "the Second Death," as Revelation 20:14 and 21:8 illumine it. Those consigned to the flames of torment are seen to be outside the celestial Body of Christ, or Kingdom of God. As further revealed in I Corinthians 6:9, 10 and Revelation 22:15, they consist of "dogs, sorcerers, idolaters, fornicators, adulterers [certain sex deviates], thieves, the covetous, drunkards, revilers, extortioners, and whosoever loveth and maketh a lie." (Cf. also I Timothy 1:9, 10 and Ephesians 5:5.) These are not annihilated in literal terms, but instead brought into subjugation to Christ through a process of divine judgments, otherwise spoken of as "the rod of iron" and "the sharp sword out of His mouth." For it is exactly thus—through the fiery torment of suffering—the Son Himself learned obedience.— Hebrews 5:5-10.

The torment which is eonian is hence considerably less than life itself in the true divine sense and meaning which can only comprehend *the Life that is in the Son!* In divine terms, it is not even remotely considered life in any sense, for it is life in torment and judgment; life under the divine lash; life in which the "rule of the rod of iron" prevails. Yet, because it is divinely corrective and constructive all the way through, and not altogether punitive and penal, it will in the end purify and purge, rehabilitate and redeem. The means of redemption will bring all men to their knees in all-out submission, in absolute subjection, in willing and instinctive obedience to the will of the Son and, it follows, in instant adoration of the matchless Holy Name, LORD JESUS CHRIST. Separation from the Life of the Son *is* death! Hence, "the Second Death" will at some time, in the long continuing eons ahead, come to an end, when it reaches the consummation [Gr. *telos,* "end"], even as I Corinthians 15: 26 tells us.

Therefore, both eonian life and eonian punishment, which coexist chronologically, have a stopping or cutting-off point, representing the critical juncture which winds up one cycle of eons and ushers in the next cycle of continuing eons. It is limited, however, in that when the consummation of all things is reached, which is the end of the first cycle (*now in progress*), the Son's invisible eonian reign in the Kingdom of the Heavens (namely, His Messianic Kingdom) will have been finished and He Himself then revert to a subject-status. At that point *all men* in the torment and purgatory of eonian condemnation and judgment will have acknowledged the Sonship of the Lord's *crucified* Christ, and at that point there will at last be universal reconciliation, bringing with it the triumph of harmony, peace, rest, love and restoration throughout God's tremendous universe.

Accordingly, "when all things shall be subdued unto the

Son"; "when He shall have put down all rule and all authority and power"; "when He shall have delivered up the Kingdom to *God, even the Father*"—at that exact point (the "end") *God Himself* will be supreme in His universe once more and will be ALL-IN-ALL to *all* His creatures: *all* that are in heaven, and *all* that are on earth, and *all* that are under the earth. Amen and Amen.—Philippians 2:9-11 and I Corinthians 15:24-28; with which cp. Revelation 19:14-16; 12:5 and 2:26, 27.

II

The Celestial Body of Christ Constituted

13. A.D. 31 the Anchor Leg of the Body of Christ

THE ANCHOR POINT TO WHICH THE ESTABLISHMENT OF THE celestial Body of Christ is firmly, inexorably and infallibly fixed is (as the preceding evidences) identified with the event of the resurrection out of their graves of the four Zoa and twenty-four Presbyters and their ascension to glory; the initial complement of the twofold gleaning of Pentecostal Firstfruits and the first units of humanity ever to arrive into the blessed portals called Heaven, otherwise the Kingdom of God.

It is this event which constitutes *per se* the firm and unshakable backbone, or foundation, to which THE CHURCH OF THE FIRSTBORN, namely, "Christ the Firstfruits," is anchored. It is this event which constitutes the one sure landmark in all Christian history that for all time to come is fixed beyond question or doubt as the blessed beginning of the *Living Church* of Jesus Christ the *Risen* Lord, and thus of THE *LIVING* BODY OF CHRIST! Nor do we mean the nominal churches of Christendom which use the alias of the Name of Christ; some to exalt His teachings and the Holy Name; others as a pretense, who brazenly misrepresent that Name and who subvert and pervert the doctrine of Christ as embodied in the Sermon on the Mount and the Golden Rule. The Living Church of the Ascended Redeemer is indeed a *celestial* Body—a celestial vine with celestial roots and branches; a celestial organism having all-celestial parts.

It is the single event which, with the close of the season expressly allotted to the double plucking of Firstfruits and comprehending the calendar duration of fifty days, ushered in the fullness of the Day of Pentecost itself and thereby marked the outpouring of the Living Christ in the personal manifestation of Himself as reflected in the appearance of "cloven tongues like as of fire."—II Corinthians 3:17.

Thus the work of sealing began, as this related to the identification of those comprehended in the second plucking. The reaping itself was to occur forty years later, and would result in sifting out from the final harvest reaping—itself embracing all twelve tribes of Israel in their two houses— those who were to be denominated "out-resurrected" and who would thus constitute the complementary batch of Pentecostal Firstfruits necessary to fill out the initial quota of the same—the two Wave Loaves of the fiftieth day added to the Wave Sheaf offering of the first day. And it is these, the 144,000 embracing the two houses of Judah and Israel, who were to be the foundation stones in His gloriously fashioned celestial Body. They would not be just dead stones shrouded and sleeping in a graveyard but would be even "as lively stones built into a spiritual house," to wit, the celestial Church of Jesus Christ the Lord. They were those who were selected out of the Apostolic Generation and "sealed with the Holy Spirit of promise unto the day of redemption [*the New Birth*] of the purchased possession."—Ephesians 1:13, 14; 4:30 and cf. Matthew 24:40, 41; Luke 17:34-36.

As therefore tied to the memorable year of grace A.D. 31, divinely proclaimed to be "noted in the Scripture of truth!", *the LIVING Church of Christ* unquestionably—yea, "verily, verily"—then began its history and tradition. It was divinely scheduled so to begin under the Levitical types where it was enshrined as a *celestial* Body in glory. And in all the nineteen centuries since its celestial history and development, it has been gloriously functioning and growing (through earthly "birth" accretions) *day after day* as any living organism should and must and always does.

14. The Headship in the Body of Christ

In any consideration of this question, we have to begin with the constituent elements forming that Headship before we can safely arrive at a correct understanding of the successive categories or orders going into the Body proper. As the head in the physical body is the administrative center, control tower, and focal seat of government, with both external and internal divisions and organs (the brain, consisting of cerebrum and cerebellum, the eyes, the ears, the nose, the mouth, etc.), so is the Headship the governing medium and functional authority in the living organism which is the celestial Body of Christ.

However these may be distributed and in whatever position posted, the Headship structure in this celestial Body belongs exclusively to "Christ the Firstfruits." It is formed of that indivisible whole, comprising the "Church of the First-born," divinely pegged to the Feast of Pentecost as occurring in A.D. 31 and hence historically belonging to the Apostolic Era. The Headship consists of the Lamb, who in His own proper person and divine right is "the *Head* over all things to the *ekklesia*—or church—which is His Body," together with the Headquarters Company (group or body-guard) "who follow the Lamb *whithersoever* He goeth." —Ephesians 1:22, 23; Revelation 14:4. Therefore, no subsequent group of Christian believers, in their blindness, arrogance or presumption, can either displace and usurp the firstfruits, or by any means successfully nominate themselves into the Headship position.

To reiterate: in the Headship of Christ we have the following constituents divinely allocated therein: 1) the Lamb Himself, as Supreme Head; 2) the four Zoa and twenty-four Presbyters of Old Testament origin and identification—the Elect of grace from the ranks of the patriarchs and prophets; and 3) the 144,000 redeemed ones apostolically bracketed who, being "out-resurrected" from the twelve tribes constituting ethnic or literal Israel in their two houses, are thus classed as the Hebrew Manchild.—Colossians 1:18; Revelation 7:4-8 and 12:1-5.

The Headship in the Body of Christ, moreover, carries with it the clear and unalterable distinction and the special preferment of being divine assistants and rulers in the celestial economy pertaining to the Kingdom of the Heavens: this being, in short, *the Messianic Kingdom of the Son* and as such representing the Kingdom rule of Christ in the dominion of the heavenlies, as presented in Revelation 19:15; 11:17, 18; Daniel 7:13, 14 and 2:35, 44.

Accordingly, in this invisible domain, He fills the divine spotlight as "KING OF KINGS AND LORD OF LORDS, where [in the current cycle of eons] He is indubitably ruling the nations with a rod of iron [the Scepter of His authority] and smiting them with a sharp sword [*the Word of His authority*] which goeth out of His mouth."

The foregoing calls attention to the era of the Hereafter and to the divine punishment meted out to those who at death pass into the realm of Judgment to pay for the misdeeds done in the flesh. There they begin to learn the hard and painful (*but nevertheless divine*) way the meaning of charity, peace, goodwill, truth, mercy, pity, neighborliness, and godliness and, most important, that the best code of operation for all peoples is always the Golden Rule. This ruling and smiting of the nations at once spotlights the eonian damnation—the equivalent of Purgatory and Hellfire—to which peoples of all nations, out of every race, color, creed, and tongue, are unmistakably subjected as death comes. It is thus seen to be reformatory and redemptive in purpose and duration, and in the end inevitably brings reconciliation and salvation. And as further called to our attention in Revelation 12:5; 2:26, 27 and 14:4, those in the Headship of Christ, none other than His own apostolic Firstfruits, assist in this glorious work of reform and redemption as celestial administrators, being armed with the same scepter of authority which "the rod of iron" combined with "the Sword of the Spirit" represents.

The nations thus smitten and ruled in the Kingdom of the Son with eonian fire and torment are hence those outside the Body of Christ, constituting the rebellious, unruly, disobedient and wicked types of unregenerate humanity whom we find mentioned in Revelation 22:5; 21:8 and I Corinthians 6:9. 10. They are the unrepentant and unsaved children of wrath who compose the throng of the Great Unwashed. These are indeed ruled, disciplined, and effectively taught the way of righteousness and holiness "with a rod of iron," leading to the ultimate reconciliation and salvation of all mankind. Such a rule (or reign) specifically relates, as previously brought to light in our Topic No. 12 under "The 'Eons'", to the Hereafter and the invisible Judgment which follows the hour that tolls the mortal doom of each human being. (See also Philippians 2:10, 11; I Corinthians 15:24, 25; Hebrews 9:27; I Peter 4:17 and I Corthinians 3:13. Cf. further Jeremiah 3:15; Isaiah 29:24; 26:9 and 40:3-5.)

15. The Body of Christ Proper

As distinguished from this all-Hebrew administrative set-up, the Body of Christ Proper (in its great exterior and interior dimensions and its marvellously wonderful diversification and construction, including limbs, torso, heart, lungs, liver, kidneys, stomach, etc.) requires celestial placement of its various components and units by exact divine determination, in keeping with their functional arrangement and organic design—each one different! In this connection, see Romans 12:4, 5 and I Corinthians 12:12-18. Coming in point of order and time *after* "Christ the Firstfruits" (who thus, as previously seen, being apostolically dated, enjoy the clear divine precedence and pre-eminent status of celestial administrators in the invisible heavenly economy), and hence altogether applying to the "nations" at large, the subsequent constituents entering into the Body of Christ Proper therefore become historically bracketed *after the apostolic era.*

Thus in the present epoch of grace allotted to the un-circumcised "nations" (or Gentiles), we have a new order of things—*novus ordo seclorum!*[1] Hence there is an entirely New Creation in Him, of divine formation and derivation and of a celestial order and nature, which is dated from A.D. 70. Thereafter, "every man in his own order" will enter the Body under the allotment of the current ages or eons until the consummation of all things is reached, when His glorious Body becomes filled out and is finished. Death as a means of transmission, otherwise being the transmission belt from earth to glory, will then no longer be necessary, hence abolished! And this, of course, applies to what we now call natural death as well as to what is divinely called the *Second Death*—the latter embracing the era of eonian torment and punishment in the Hereafter, which divinely leads to refor-mation and transformation and to reconciliation and redemp-tion.

We note at this point that the word the Apostle Paul uses in the Greek (*tagma*—order), in its military connotation expresses the idea of orderly progression and sequence as exhibited in the marching order of troops, consisting of series and ranks and representing companies, battalions, etc. Hence it is that coming into the Body of Christ *at death* (which is the New Birth), "every man is to be in his own exact sequential order," where each member is "set as it pleaseth God"—being a divine operation which, for the be-liever, unfolds *the extension of salvation*—until the fullness of the Body is reached. "*Then* cometh the end [Gr. *telos,* namely, the consummation of all things], when the Kingdom is delivered up to God, even the Father . . . when the Son also Himself shall be subject unto HIM [the Father] that

---

[1] The Great Seal of the United States (officially adopted June 20, 1782) bears on one side this Latin inscription which, in connection with the birth of the nation, calls attention to the institution of "a new series of ages"—literally, "*a new order of things*" in the political picture then existing. As introduced in the above discussion, it has the same meaning.

put all things under Him, *that God may be ALL-IN-ALL!*"
(I Corinthians 15:20-51 and cp. Romans 12:4, 5 and I Corinthians 12:12-18.)

16. The Gospel-Age Resurrection Harvest

We discover from the foregoing references that inasmuch
as there are many types of celestial bodies—there being
"one glory of the sun, and another glory of the moon, and
another glory of the stars," and even as "one star differeth
from another star in glory,"—even so, in the invisible realm
of the celestial Body of Christ as now constituted and as
now currently functioning in the heavenlies above, the begotten entity (corresponding to the old Adamic "soul" and
divinely created to replace it, and called by Paul "bare or
naked grain," from the Gr. *gumnon-kokkon,* literally "naked
cocoon or uncovered germ of life") which constitutes the believer's "other self" (hence the cocoon or kernel, the inner
core or nucleus, the *germ,* of his celestial identity), has bestowed upon it a celestial-type body which it inherits at the
instant hour of death and which, not being flesh and blood
and bones, is its heavenly mansion. It is therefore seen to
be something entirely new in the nature of a body, by way
of a divine gift, "such as it pleaseth the Father to give it;
and hence to every seed [i.e., the naked grain or germ which
is the *begotten or new spirit* within the believer] its own
type celestial body."—I Corinthians 15:35-50; John 14:1-3
and II Corinthians 5:1-4.

And this, in divine terms and exposition, is what "the
resurrection of the dead" means in the present faith era
and economy of grace. In brief, this is the present Gospel-
age resurrection harvest in which *all true believers in Him*
share and share alike, becoming beneficiaries in the Great
Adventure which comes with the occasion and at the instant of mortal death in the flesh—the New Creation arising
immediately out of the old, which is its birth; *namely, the
New Birth!* And the key to the mystery of the Hereafter
and to this invisible realization, which is the resurrection
to life, is the *begettal again,* without which no man can see

the Father's face or enter (by translation and redemption) "into the Kingdom of His dear Son." "*Verily*," says Jesus, "*ye must be begotten again!*"—John 3:3-7; Colossians 1:13.

In this Gospel-age resurrection, no element, constituent, ingredient, component, or particle of the old Adamic structure, however minute or microscopic, can find any place in the celestial Body of Christ. Neither any flesh nor any bones, and certainly none of its blood, and none of its nature (including its affections and lusts) can exist: in short, none of the old creation belongs! The believer becomes, and is therefore *a new creature* indeed. Hence, being *new* in this divine sense spells the complete elimination of all that is old in the first Adam—and all connected with it! As Paul puts it, "flesh and blood cannot inherit the Kingdom of God [which in divine terms is THE BODY OF CHRIST], neither doth corruption inherit incorruption." This quite effectively disposes of the notion that the New Creation in Christ Jesus can mean something that is part old in the first Adam plus something else that is part new in the second Adam. "Therefore if any man be in Christ, *he is a New Creature*: old things are passed away; behold ALL THINGS are become new!"—II Corinthians 5:17 and cp. Matthew 9:17 and Luke 5:37, 38.

17. *The Symbolism of Baptism*[2]

Significantly enough, baptism is the Christian ordinance whose ritual meaning and practice correctly interprets and

---

[2] Baptism in the sense of immersion expresses "the New Birth." This is not to say, however, that water baptism is the only valid Christian formula which can express this meaning. The baptism of John, though consummated under water in the River Jordan, was nonetheless inferior to the baptism of the Holy Spirit, which doesn't have to be under water, and which John the Baptist and the Apostle Paul both recognized and Jesus Himself underscored. (Cf. Matthew 3:11, 12; John 3:28, 30; I Corinthians 1:12-17; and Acts 1:5.) Any formula which by its accepted usage and interpretation expresses the concept of burial, thereby expresses the meaning of complete immersion, and is therefore wholly acceptable to God, seeing that "*God is SPIRIT* and seeketh worshippers who will worship Him in spirit and in truth."—John 4:23, 24; cp. II Corinthians 3:6.

proclaims this message of the New Creation, the coming into
being and existence via the New Birth. The rite of immersion
(or burial) is the divinely ordained symbol that exactly expresses the elimination of all that is in, and connected with,
the old Adam in favor of something better, something completely new, to be obtained *through grace* in the Second
Adam. In Christian experience, therefore, baptism clearly
reflects and focusses the mystery of the New Birth in terms
of what really takes place with every believer at death. It
expresses exactly the complete demise, elimination, obliter-
ation and annihilation of the old Adamic man in the totality
of its structure and nature and its physical composition and
soulish aspects; all this being comprehended in its flesh and
blood and bones as presently constituted. In relation to the
old Adamic carcass which is ceremoniously put away with
appropriate and solemn funeral rites in some graveyard at
death, baptism correctly tells us that it is something to be
gotten rid of, to be buried out of sight, *and this for keeps!*

Like the fabled bird, the phoenix of old arising out of its
own ashes to become newborn, thus renewing itself into a
continued state of animated existence, the New Creature in
Christ Jesus that becomes literally "born" out of the old at
death similarly arises to inherit its new redemption body
which descends from heaven, thus to take its place organically in the celestial Body of Christ, which is the Kingdom of
God. "Therefore we are buried with Him by baptism *into
death*: that like as Christ was raised up from the dead
[whereby to become the Firstborn from the dead] by the
glory of the Father, even so we also should walk in newness
of life."—Romans 6:3, 4.

Being completely dead in this anticipatory sense and rid
of our fleshly Adamic carcasses of sin explains how we have
the indwelling life of the risen Son *imputed and reckoned*
to us through a literal transfer from Him to us, which further explains the mystery of the Begettal through "the
power of His Resurrection." And the secret of it all, as expressed in John 15:5, is the *Living Christ* who comes into

every believer by His indwelling Presence. It is His Life we are henceforth to live, which the symbolism of baptism mightily expresses and which in turn becomes imputed (meaning literally transferred and thus *infused*) to us. It is His Life, attributed to the believer, which establishes a new literal identity for him, called the "begettal again."

It is the portion of the Living Christ—the essence in the Vine—which thus resides within the believer, who becomes identified as the branch. Christ's own resurrected identity (including His life, His righteousness, His immortality, even all His attributes) becomes transferred, attributed, imputed, transfused, call it whatever you will, and thus becomes the believer's "other self." The Vine is therefore in the branch and conversely the branch is in the Vine. The believer is henceforth *justified by faith*, a divine arrangement which, being premised on the fact of his symbolical death, compensates for any apparent or obvious defects, shortcomings, weaknesses, and mistakes (as man views such things), and which thus brings the believer up to the same correct standards of perfection and obedience possessed by the Living Christ Himself. And this in essence is the meaning of justification by faith.

Accordingly, the Living Christ within—being *begotten* into the believer's inward parts—becomes in reality "the *spirit* (nucleus, germ, or embryo) of a just man" (or one justified by faith) who has yet to be "*made perfect*" (i.e., complete and whole with a body) at his "birth."—Romans 6:3-11; 4:6-8, 22-24; James 2:23; Hebrews 12:23.

As far as successful Christian experience and genuine Christian living go, our present status as believers is reckoned as "adoption" until at death sonship becomes manifest in terms of actual "birth." The period of the adoption consequently corresponds to the pre-natal state of the believer in grace, this being the period of his spiritual gestation. Actual sonship then comes at "birth," which in divine terms is "the manifestation of the sons of God." Thus, in order to achieve the status of adopted son in our present Adamic state of

existence, the believer must crucify the old man—with all his
organic and functional characteristics as well as the soulish
and sinful propensities embracing his deeds, affections, and
lusts—and this the symbolism of baptism effectively evidences in our regeneration.

Only in this sense is the believer accounted an adopted
son, a state he temporarily acquires through the burial rite
of baptism in acknowledgment that he has yet to go through
a period of *waiting* (gestation) before true sonship is literally acquired. It is a period in which, in terms of spiritual
biology, he has to wait until the manifestation of sonship
becomes a living reality. The Apostle Paul discourses on this
theme eloquently in Romans 8, where he draws the distinction between the status of adopted children and "the manifestation of the sons of God," showing the former to be
constructive and tentative whereas the latter is only an
"earnest expectation" which has to be actively "waited for."
In verses 24 and 25 he writes: "For we are saved by hope:
but hope that is seen is not hope, for what a man seeth why
doth he yet hope for? But if we hope for that we see not,
then do we with patience wait for it."

Reading I John 3:1-3 with some degree of spiritual
discernment, we find the same thought trenchantly re-
peated which is in harmony with Paul's own line of faultless
reasoning:

> "1) Behold, what manner of love the Father hath be-
> stowed upon us, that we should be called the sons of God
> [namely, through adoption]: therefore the world knoweth
> us not, because it knew Him not. 2) Beloved, *NOW are we
> the SONS of God,* and it does not yet appear what we shall
> be: but we know that, when He shall appear, we shall be
> like Him; for [then] we shall see Him as He is. 3) And every
> man that hath this *hope* in him purifieth himself, even as He
> is pure."

In the sense of adopted son, the believer is said to be
born; whereas in the sense of manifested son, the believer is

only begotten; and this is the clear divine distinction that both Paul and John are making. Adoption is constructive; manifestation is the real article, which is actual sonship. In adoption, the final result is approached through a figure of speech which anticipates it and thus introduces it as an already accomplished fact.

Accordingly, in Romans 4:16-25, Paul declares that "Abraham considered his own body to be dead when he was about an hundred years old," being like-minded concerning his wife Sarah's womb—which was dead, too! Yet Abraham was called a *father,* indeed, "the father of many nations," by the One in whom he believed, *"even God who quickeneth the dead, and calleth those things which be not as though they were."* The sole basis of sonship thus lies in the believer's hope, which is the active reflection and expression of an invincible faith, the sort of faith that was a glorious moment for Abraham who "staggered not at the promise of God through unbelief; but was *strong in faith,* giving glory to God, and being fully persuaded that what He had promised, He was able also to perform: and therefore it was imputed to him for righteousness."

Consequently, we find the Apostle enjoining us to "reckon yourselves to be dead indeed unto sin, but alive unto God [as adopted sons] through Jesus Christ our Lord." Also he admonishes: "And they that are Christ's [being "had" and begotten] have crucified the flesh [of which baptism becomes the transparent symbol] with the affections and lusts."—Romans 6:11 and Galatians 5:24.

"So then they that are in the flesh cannot please God. But ye are not in the flesh but in the Spirit [being begotten], if so be THE SPIRIT OF GOD [the imaged Christ *Himself*] dwell in you. Now if any man have not the Spirit of Christ [and is therefore not begotten again], He is none of His. And if *Christ be in you* [expressing the literal product and fruit of the Begettal; hence the begotten entity itself—the vital embryo *in utero*—which reflects the imaged Christ, this

being the New Creature and the believer's *other self*], the
body is dead because of sin but the Spirit is life because of
righteousness [here expressing, in terms of symbolism, the
twofold transaction—*death and newness of life*—which at
once gives baptism its particular significance]. But if the
Spirit of Him that raised up Jesus *dwell in you* [again expressing the evidence of the Begettal], He that raised up
Christ from the dead [to become the Firstborn, henceforth
the Living Christ] shall also *quicken* [expressing the follow-
up in the Begettal] your mortal bodies *by His Spirit that
dwelleth in you.*"—Romans 8:8-11.

As clearly seen in the foregoing, both the begettal and
the quickening which follows it give infallible witness to
"the Power of His Resurrection" as gloriously wrought in
the believer, whereby *the Life of the Son* in all its fullness
and literalness becomes generated. Hence, as a result of
the Resurrection's overshadowing power, the believer, like
Mary, "finds himself begotten with child of the Holy Spirit":
in both cases, this being literally, "Christ in you!" And it is
the fact of this *new creation* which the Christian rite of baptism, in its multiple forms, so vitally expresses in the sublime and generating meaning of its compelling symbolism.
—Luke 1:35; Matthew 1:18-21 and I John 5:9-12.

18. *Justification by Faith*

It is in the vital relationship existing between the Vine
and the branches, in the biological aspect, that we obtain
the literal reality and fruits of the operation of the doctrine
of justification by faith. Carried to its ultimate conclusion
it is the complete and satisfying explanation of the mystery
of the New Creation, whereby all the elements and ingre-
dients which form the whole of the New Creature are entirely derived outside the believer's present earthly frame
and milieu. In short, both the New Spirit (the counterpart
to the old Adamic soul) and the new celestial body itself
(the counterpart to the old Adamic carcass consisting of

flesh and blood and bones) which the believer inherits are the free gifts of God to him through Jesus Christ. In this consideration of the question, as we have hitherto seen, we are of course dealing with something that is completely new: for "ALL the old things are passed away."—II Corinthians 5:17.

To begin with, the old Adamic soul becomes replaced (beginning in this present state of mortal existence) with its celestial counterpart, the new spirit-nucleus or germ identified as the portion of the Indwelling Presence of the Living Christ Himself, which as invisible "Divine Fire" or emanation comes in to abide with the believer forever if he wants it. This, in spiritual terms, is the New Begettal, or pre-natal state of the believer, because of the fact that a new life thus becomes initiated. Next, the new "spirit-soul" in its biological evolution, which occurs *only at death,* is "made perfect" with a new body which descends from heaven. And presto, the New Birth and the New Creation itself are both accomplished facts and literal realities! Only justification by faith makes this at all possible, and only "the Power of His Resurrection" can work this miracle! Accordingly, only through justification by faith (which includes within its scope "the Power of His Resurrection") do we have the full and definitive answer to the question raised in I Corinthians 15:35: "How are the dead raised up with what body do they come?"

Thus, carried to its ultimate conclusion, the simple meaning of justification by faith is itself the divinely convincing explanation of the believer's *perfection* (his completeness which makes him a whole New Man) at death, with the Father's gift of a celestial-type body from His own heavenly storehouse.—John 14:1-4; II Corinthians 5:1-4 and I Corinthians 15:38. Along with this vital concept, perhaps our readers can now also sense the significance of the Vine together with its branches, which enables the begotten believer truly to declare: "Because He is in me, I am in Him; and because my life is *hid* in Him, I have His Life. And because

He is mine, I am also His. Therefore, even as He is, so am I.
I am whatever He is; and whatever He has, I have. All, all
are mine! Therefore, because He lives, I too live—*hence can
never die*. And because He is immortal, I too am immortal."

It's as simple as that. In short, whatever is true of the
Vine is likewise bound to be true of its branches, both being
indivisible in their reciprocal union and vital relationship.

In relation to the Source, namely, the Vine, the believer
has everything; apart from the Source, he has nothing. In relation to the Source, he has life, righteousness, immortality,
power, light, all of which are said to be "hid with Christ in
God" for him.—Colossians 3:3, 4. Hence, it follows that when
Christ comes in (the premise being that the believer is
dead), then everything in Christ comes in, too—His life, His
light, His righteousness, even His immortality. It follows
further that unless Christ comes in, the believer has absolutely nothing; he has nothing of which to boast except his
own self-righteousness, which being "an unclean thing is as
filthy rags."—Isaiah 64:6.

And this is what gives point to Paul's dissertation in Romans 3, which makes it plain that "by *the deeds of the law*
there shall no flesh be justified in His sight" (v. 20); that the
lone requisite for salvation comes as the result of "being
justified freely by His grace through the redemption that
is in Christ Jesus" (v. 24); and further, that in the believer's
natural circumstances where he is helpless and undone,
naked and unclean and filthy, the only righteousness he can
have is the righteousness he obtains through the Begettal,
when Christ comes in! Thus Paul makes the point of "declaring the righteousness of Christ Jesus which alone can
provide remission of sins that are past, through the forbear-
ance of God" (v. 25). By way of further emphasis: "to declare, as he says *at this time,* His righteousness: that He
might be just and the justifier of him which believeth in
Jesus" (v. 26).

It is in this sense, accordingly, that we are to ponder the

instructions given by the Divine Teacher Himself in Matthew 6:33: to "seek ye first *the Kingdom of God and His righteousness.*" The divine assurance is that, from there on, all necessary and pertinent material considerations will be taken care of. It is in this sense, moreover, that Christians will find, when at last they discover the meaning of the Kingdom of God in relation to the Begettal and the New Birth, that they will automatically "cease and desist" going about *establishing their own brand of righteousness* and putting a wholly false emphasis on "the deeds of the law," all of which constitute a form of pseudo-religion. In this connection, and for the benefit of those who stress legalism as a necessary adjunct in the divine program of salvation, Paul writes: "For I bear them record that they have a zeal of God, but not according to knowledge. For they being ignorant of God's Righteousness, and going about to establish their own righteousness, have not submitted themselves unto the righteousness of God."—Romans 10:2, 3.

Thus the Apostle explains our topic in terms of "the Righteousness of God which is by faith of Jesus Christ unto all and upon all them that believe."—Romans 3:22. He next follows through, in Romans 6:1-11, with a further analysis of justification which he gives in terms of the meaning of baptism, wherein "being planted together in the likeness of His death, we shall be also [raised] in the likeness of His resurrection . . . knowing that Christ being raised from the dead dieth no more, death hath no more dominion over Him." Even so does justification by faith teach the same lesson which reflects itself in the quickening of "a lively hope" begotten into the believer's inward parts; consequently, *death hath no more dominion over the believer either!*

In the context of the foregoing, we can now confidently accept the conclusion found in Romans 5:1, 2: "Therefore being justified by faith, we have peace with God through our Lord Jesus Christ: by whom we have access by faith into this grace wherein we stand, and rejoice in *hope of the glory of God*," which consequently takes us into "celestial places, to dwell together with Him."—Ephesians 1:3.

In Colossians 1:23-27, this "hope of the Gospel [identical with the hope of the glory of God] . . . whereof [the Apostle declares] I Paul am made a minister" is tied in to "the mystery which hath been hid from ages and from generations, but now is made manifest to His saints: to whom God would make known what is the riches of the *glory* of this mystery among the Gentiles [namely, all the nations without distinction of origin or fleshly descent or race or color or creed, the circumcised and uncircumcised alike], which is *Christ in you, the hope of Glory!*"

Needless to say, what the Apostle is actually saying here is more than meets the eye. He is correlating justification by faith with the New Begettal ("Christ in you"), showing the former to be a living active concept concerned with the believer's faith which in turn actually generates within the believer concerned *a literal new identity.* This wonderful new identity (make no mistake about it!) is Christ's very own Presence and Life, now divinely said to be the believer's, and which thus makes the begotten identity of the one the exact identity and image of the other, the resultant product being "Christ in you!"

Henceforth, realizing the very definite and literal existence of the new entity or identity brought about through an act of divine creation, Paul was more than ever conscious of the fact that he was "crucified with Christ," which the symbolism of baptism particularly stressed for him. He was thus able to declare in Galatians 2:20, "nevertheless I live, *yet not I, but Christ liveth in me;* and the life which I now live in the flesh [meaning Paul's other self which now lives in his old Adamic carcass] I live by the faith of the Son of God." The new Paul is acknowledging the existence of *the Life of the Son* in him, since he as the old Paul is crucified and dead, and is thus acknowledging that it is the Life of the Indwelling Christ which is now living in him, instead of Paul's old self. Consequently, the old Paul is dead, and the new Paul is "Christ in you, the hope of glory!" And since it is "by the faith of the Son of God" that Paul has this new life, he is recognizing the fact that it is justification by faith which not only introduces it initially through the Divine Begettal (the penetration of the Indwelling Presence), but manifests it also through "the Power of His Resurrection."

Accordingly, Paul shows a clear appreciation and recognition of the fact that he must no longer reckon himself as Paul (being the party of the first Adam), but instead in terms of Him who is His actual life (being the party who *is* the Second Adam) and, as such, "a quickening Spirit," and who thus becomes the progenitor of an entirely literal New Creation. In terms of the Living Christ Himself, Paul's own life as the New Creature begins, marking the begettal of his "other self."

In Colossians 3:1-4, the Apostle further makes it clear that because the believer through the ceremonial rite of baptism has "reckoned himself dead," which in effect discontinues his identity in the first Adam and at once gives him status and entrée into the Second Adam through the correlative processes of regeneration, he therefore acquires the "Life hid with Christ in God." Being inherent in the Living Christ Himself, it is now the believer's by a spiritual process of transfusion and infusion, because through faith he is divinely justified. Starting out from the premise "If ye be risen with Christ," the Apostle pursues the idea and meaning of baptism: "For ye are dead, and *your life is hid with Christ in God. When Christ who is our Life* shall appear [same occurring at the New Birth, when we are *born* into celestial sonship], then shall ye also appear with Him in glory."—Colossians 1:3, 4.

The conclusion is therefore inescapable, from the premise previously established in Romans 3:24-26, that the believer's new identity (or rather his other self) is completely *derivative,* in the sense of its being something distinctly apart from himself, and therefore quite outside and exclusive of his old Adamic being, personality, and nature—being, in short, the

Adamic ego. Consequently, using the analogy which Jesus Himself gives, as the branch is to the vine so is the believer to Christ. The branch is an inherent, integral, and indivisible part of the vine's economy (its substance, nature, and identity) and from it is derived the branch's sustenance and its very life essence (the sap). Likewise does the believer derive his very own substance, nature, and vitality, even his eonian life, his immortality, his divine nature and identity, completely from the Indwelling Presence of the Living Christ Himself who thus regenerates him, bringing into perspective the new potentialities which are now *his very own*, both prospectively and literally.

The divine life with its inherent immortality, together with all the inherent potentialities and celestial factors of the divine nature itself, now becomes imputed, attributed, transferred, credited, and reckoned to the believer, and is hence the heart and the ultimate expression of the doctrine of justification by faith. Note carefully that it is only on the basis of God's righteousness and the corollary premise of the believer's being dead that justification by faith can deliver to the believer Christ's very own literal Life. This Life includes all that belongs to Christ Himself and, of course, the attributes of His divinity; namely, His righteousness, His light, His immortality, His celestial power and glory. Reduced to lowest terms, justification by faith is, in effect, a *Deed of Assignment* from Him to us, signed, sealed and delivered!

19. *"Ye are Complete in Him"*

We approach this topic in the knowledge that the Heavenly Father Himself supplies everything necessary to salvation through "Jesus Christ the crucified, risen, and ascended Lord"; being "complete in Him." We know also that inasmuch as the believer's new life and his new estate are "hid with Christ in God," they must therefore be derived from this one heavenly Source. This is all that is necessary to explain how the New Creation comes into being; through elimination of the old in order to provide room for the new, which comes in to supplant it. "Therefore if any man be in Christ [where the believer's new life and his new estate are hid and where same are also complete in Him], he is a New Creature: old things are passed away [hence completely eliminated]: *behold, all things are become new!"*— II Corinthians 5:17.

Recognizing the divine Source of the believer's new life, the positive revelation becomes unfolded through Paul that *"ye are complete in Him,* which is the Head of all principality and power."—Colossians 2:10. In other words, the new spirit (let us call it the new soul) and the new body of the believer together are *both* "complete in Him"—fabricated and fashioned for us by Him, and ready for delivery to the believer at the instant of the "birth" called death. And that is why it is distinctly declared, in three places, that "in the Father's celestial house, there are many mansions" (John 14:2); that *at death* "the Father giveth to each new soul a body as it hath pleased Him" (I Corinthians 15:38); and that there is "a building of God, an house not made with hands, eonian in the heavens: hence being our house which is from heaven" (II Corinthians 5:1, 2).

Before birth, there must certainly be begettal, which at once provides the key for entrance into the Kingdom of God together with the glorious inheritance of celestial bodies which goes with that entrance. In turn, this begettal opens the door to the understanding of our "completeness in Christ." And this the Apostle goes on to illustrate in the symbolism of baptism when, in the continuation of his theme, he explains (Colossians 2:11-13) that although uncircumcised in flesh, nevertheless *"ye are circumcised* with the circumcision made without hands in putting off the body of the sins of the flesh by the circumcision of Christ [which itself is seen as an outflow of justification by faith, whereby circumcision is also imputed, attributed, and reckoned to the believer]: buried with Him in baptism, wherein also ye are raised with Him from the dead. And you, being dead in your sins and the uncircumcision of your flesh hath He *quickened* [the follow-up and infallible witness of the begettal] together with Him, having forgiven you all trespasses."

Thus through the New Begettal, followed in due course of events with the New Birth itself, does every believer in Christ acquire *"completeness in Him."* From Him also he acquires his new "spirit-soul" (the celestial core and divine basis of his new life and personality identity) together with his new celestial body, both of which it takes to complete the New Creation. Being "complete in Him" thus provides the believer with his two-part celestial inheritance: 1) his celestial new soul (embryo, germ, spirit-nucleus, or ego) constituting the beginning of his new identity; and 2) his celestial-type body, divinely suitable for the Hereafter in the Kingdom of God and hence necessary for dwelling together with Him in heavenly places—*both the free gifts of God to man!*—Romans 5:15-17; 6:23; Hebrews 12:23 and I Corinthians 15:38.

20. *"The Power of His Resurrection"*

In consonance with his own revelation of the meaning of justification, Paul makes it plain that he was determined to forego many of the substantial earthly rights to which he was divinely entitled, that he might win for himself "completeness in Christ." Hence, for Paul, it was the privilege of inheriting *in Him* a literal, completely new spirit as well as a literal, completely new celestial body. Accordingly, in Philippians 3:7-10, he writes:

> "But what things were gain to me, them I counted loss for Christ. Yea, doubtless, and I count all things but loss for the excellency of the knowledge of Christ Jesus my Lord: for whom I have suffered the loss of all things, and do count them but dung, that I may win Christ, and be found in Him, not having my own righteousness which is of the law, *but that which is through the faith of Christ, the righteousness*

which is of God through faith: that I may know Him, and
the power of his Resurrection, and the fellowship of His
sufferings, being made conformable unto His death."

What Paul wanted more than all else for himself, and
was determined to achieve even at the cost of much substantial sacrifice, was the enjoyment of the experience of the
New Begettal along with its true witness. Further, of course,
the New Birth would guarantee him at the instant hour of
mortal dissolution a secure place in the *exanastasis,* or "Out-
Resurrection" of the dead, which he mentions in verse 11.
In short, to every Christian believer who has been *begotten
again,* in this literal and vital sense, this is "the Power of
His Resurrection!" It is this "power" that is directly responsible for the faith which activates the begettal of the imaged
Christ; the literal celestial embryo which is in fact the new
entity constituting the new identity of the believer, *his other
self!*

It is hence the Life of Him who, in the hour of His
victory over death and the grave and His ascended glory,
could utter these living words of comfort and assurance to
His own beloved disciple John on the Isle of Patmos. He instructed John to broadcast His words forthwith to believers
everywhere in all the *ekklesias*: "I am He that liveth, and
was dead; and, behold, I am alive forever more [Gr. to the
ages of the ages], Amen; and have the keys of *Hades* and
Thanatos [namely, the grave and death]. Write the things
which thou hast seen, and the things which are, and the
things which shall be hereafter." (Revelation 1:18, 19 and
Cp. Romans 6:9.)

It also embraces the same message of comfort and life
uttered upon an earlier occasion to Martha, then racked
with pain and misery over the death of her beloved brother
Lazarus. "Jesus said unto her, *I am the Resurrection and the
Life*: he that believeth in Me, though he were dead, yet
shall he live: and whosoever liveth and believeth in Me

shall never die. Believest thou this? She saith unto Him, Yea,
Lord, *I believe that Thou art the Christ, the Son of God,
which should come into the world.*"—John 11:25-27.

By divine revelation, Martha had been given a foretaste
of the Risen Christ and the Glory to follow, accompanied
with a penetrating insight of "the Power of His Resurrection," and had at once perceived the omnipotence of the
Living Christ when, being at last in the form of the Holy
Spirit (the *Paraclete*), He would be "lifted up" and glorified.
As her mortal senses became quickened from above with a
vision of the coming prospect, she came to the realization
that with the imminence of the Ascension and the ensuing
Glory, the Life that was the Master's would thereafter be
absolutely *hers.* By divine enlightenment, she was immediately conscious of the transference of that Life to each
and every *true* believer in Him and hence in His Almighty
Power, which for Martha and the other contemporaries of
the Apostolic Generation would be fulfilled at the set time
in Scripture for this miracle of grace to begin; namely,
A.D. 70. (John 7:38, 39; II Corinthians 3:17 and cf. John
12:32, 33 and I Peter 1:11.)

Through simply believing that this would divinely tran-
spire in her own generation, Martha had at once become
aware of the significance of the Master's words to her, comprehending as these did the ushering in of *a mighty new
order of things.* She realized that the dispensational period,
limited to the close of the apostolic era and marking God's
own dividing line between two distinct ages, would be pregnant with remarkable and profound changes in the character of God's dealing with mankind from then on.

Thus believing, which assured her of the glorious prospect of having life "more abundantly," she was overpowered
with the rapture of the begettal within her of a quite "lively
hope." And this was the knowledge and conviction that the
time was soon, even at the door, when the death-state of
unconsciousness would no longer be the inheritance of be-

lievers in the Risen Christ and in "the Power of His Resurrection"—no, not even for one minute! Indeed, where waiting in some graveyard for some far-off dispensational resurrection morn, reckoned in time, need never be their lot. She realized that their life would be both "hidden with Christ" and "complete in Him," and that the resurrected, ascended, and glorified Christ would share His blessed life with them. She believed that His abundant life would be their very own, to have and to hold in fee simple, given to them freely with no strings attached. And she moreover believed that the reality and fullness of His Divine Life would be their very own, in terms of its literal possession, to enjoy forever, because imputed to them through justification by faith and wrought within them through the Divine Begettal.—John 10:10.

Like Paul, Martha had indeed sensed the *mighty* "Power of His Resurrection"; and be it said to her everlasting credit, she did not *err* in selling short "the Power of God." Hence her glorious reward!—Matthew 22:29.

As to the personal meaning which believers are now to give to the *Second Coming of Christ* in the present era of grace and truth (this being especially the case since A.D. 70), the following utterance from a Christian pastor who has given much thoughtful and reverent attention to the matter sums it up precisely. He quite properly draws the distinction between *Eschatology* (or what will happen at the end of the world) and *Vital Christianity* (or what can happen now) and then adds:

"To me, Christianity is a very practical thing. It gets down into the pains, the aches, the hopes and fears, home, play and business, the totality of life. Everyone can enjoy a helpful personal relationship with Jesus. To me the Second Coming means, not the spectacular arrival of the Son of God on clouds of glory, but a *spiritual indwelling*. If we live in fellowship with Jesus, through prayer and the Living Word, through identification with Him and through upright living,

He will come as a spiritual presence and live within us—so we don't have to depend upon our wisdom and power. He will manifest His wisdom and strength in our lives and in our personal affairs."[3]

And this, my dear readers and friends, is what "the Power of His Resurrection" does indeed, absolutely and literally, accomplish. Truly, this is the essence of the Begettal, as brought into focus in the message of *The New Birth!*

---

[3] Dr. Clifford H. Richmond (Minister, Chevy Chase Methodist Church), as reported by Kenneth Dole in *Washington Post & Times Herald*, August 27, 1955.

III

Begotten Again
and Begettal Completed

21. *"Christ Formed in You"—the Begettal*

BY WAY OF FURTHER OPENING NEW VISTAS CONNECTED WITH
the approach to our theme, we are compelled at this juncture
to call attention to certain additional aspects of the Begettal.
And this brings us to the third thematic division of this
Bible study on *The New Birth*.

It is not surprising, after we begin to understand the
nature of the Kingdom of God as particularized in John 3:
1-12, to find the underlying emphasis in Paul's Kingdom
preaching expressed in the many changes he rings on being
begotten again. All the way through in every one of his
epistles, it shows that he has the conversation with Nicodemus in mind, to whom the subject was initially introduced
by the Divine Teacher Himself. Little wonder, therefore,
that in the intensive earnestness and persuasive enthusiasm
of the preaching of the Gospel of salvation, Paul could find
himself, as he took the occasion to state, travailing in the
pangs of "birth" (or labor) *"until Christ be formed in you!"*
—Galatians 4:19.

The mystery of this invisible formation, connoting in
Paul's own mind, as it does in the mind of every believer
who has the Witness of God in him, a *real, actual, literal and*

quite vital divine creation, is exactly what Paul speaks of in Galatians 4:19. He further calls attention to this same mystery in Colossians 1:26, 27: "even the mystery which hath been *hid* from [past] ages and from [past] generations, but *now* [in Paul's own Apostolic Generation] is made manifest to His saints: to whom God would make known what is the riches of the glory of this mystery among the Gentiles [Gr. nations]: which is *Christ in You, the Hope of Glory.*"

The new entity thus begotten and thus denominated is in fact, in its spirit-essence, development, and content as well as in its literal aspects, a portion, emanation, continuation, and *verily a copy* of the Living Christ Himself. The new identity, in the sense of its being given to the believer as a free gift, is hence imputed to him, which provides the basis of his *other self* in terms of the New Creation. As such, it entirely originates from the personality and being of the risen, ascended, and glorified Christ, as expressed in "the Power of His Resurrection." And as therefore begotten into the believer's innermost parts, it becomes an integral and living component dwelling in the midst of his old Adamic circumstances, in which it exists without being assimilated, but like any other embryo grows and grows and grows, being vitalized, nourished, and sustained by its celestial connections and heritage and by its Life from above.

Everything divinely credited to the believer in his new situation, starting from Begettal here below and continuing into his new celestial environment when he is "born," is completely *new*, which it has to be in order to be a New Creation. Thus the believer acquires his new identity, his new spirit-soul, his new celestial body, his new existence, and even (as he will discover when he gets into glory) *his new name*. And thus when he is born into the Kingdom of God, which is otherwise the celestial Body of Christ, he will find himself in perfect harmony and rapport with all other members in the environment of that organic Body, as well as in perfect union with the Head.

The analogy of the Vine and branches presented in John 15:1-9 embraces this vital relationship perfectly. The universal or cosmic Christ, from the celestial perch of His glory, sheds Himself abroad as the sevenfold Lamb. Being "the seven Spirits of God sent forth into all the earth," He manifests Himself everywhere and at once as the Omnipotent Living Christ through the Indwelling Presence of His Spirit, representing *per se* the extrusion of Himself and the radiant energy of His Omnipresence. The personality and identity of the Living Christ, with all the divine appurtenances and attributes pertaining to His celestial Being, consequently come into the believer to image itself in the formation of a new identity—and this is the Begettal! (Cf. Revelation 5:6; 4:5 and Ephesians 4:10.)

Note further that, in Revelation 3:20, the same vital concept of the Begettal is expressed, the same concept of *the Living Christ* within; namely, "Christ in You, the Hope of Glory," expressing as this does *"Christ formed in you"*. "Behold, I stand at the door and knock: if any man hear My voice and open the door, I will come in to him, and will sup with him, and He with Me."

Hence, in this vital but quite unspectacular and invisible fashion, embracing a highly privileged and distinctly personal intimate relationship, many believers become begotten and *"found with child of the Holy Spirit;"* and thus many Christs, *or copies of Him,* are formed, to conform with the original celestial pattern. And hence, in the divine trope of the true Vine and its branches, we have the exact proliferation of the *Living Christ Himself* plus the *manifold Christs* whom He begets!

22.   *The Imaged Christ the Product of the Begettal*

The imaged Christ is therefore the end result or product of the Begettal. Of course it is the same thing whether we call it the foetal or embryonic Christ, the vital or cosmic

Christ, the Indwelling or Radiant Presence, the incarnated Christ or "Christ in you,"[1] the "Seed Christ," the Divine Fire, the New Creature or New Man, the New Identity or Entity, the believer's other self, the begotten "soul," the spirit-nucleus or germ, bare grain or naked seed, or just plain "the *spirit* of the just man" who is justified by faith, or any other comparable and fitting synonym. A rose by any other name is just as sweet, this being especially true in the light of II Corinthians 3:6 and John 4:23, 24.

Hence, even the expression "immortal soul," being relative, is a quite adequate descriptive in the sense that it applies *only* to the believer begotten the divine way; to the one begotten of the Divine Fire in the initial transaction of the penetration of the Indwelling Presence. Consequently, it does not mean that he is inherently immortal of himself, but only in the sense that his immortal soul is completely derivative through justification by faith and because of the fact that he is a *true* believer. The Living Christ is the only one who is inherently immortal, which is true of Him wherever He is. In His celestial glory where He sits at the right hand of the Father's throne, it is inherent; in the believer where He comes to dwell and sup and where it is exactly attributed (which is to say, derived), it is likewise inherent even there. Being "alive forevermore," He is that wher-

---

[1] In the teaching of some, this might also be put *"Yashuah* in you" but the principle involved is nevertheless the same. And here again we need to be particularly reminded that the things of the spirit, in order for their divine meaning to be affirmatively understood and grasped, must be lifted out of the realm of semantics—namely, the use of mere words which are undoubtedly synonymous in purpose and spirit but which can sometimes be made to confuse and hide the central concept at stake, and here embracing THE SON OF GOD in terms of *"the One sent."*—John 10:36; 11:42; 12:44, 45; 17:3. Any expression, therefore, which by its usage and intent expresses this lowest common denominator is divinely acceptable; and quibbling over words is not only unseemly but wholly out of order.

ever He is, whether in heaven, in earth, or under the earth. As the Cosmic Christ, His Life, His righteousness, His immortality are indivisible from His divinity and His universality. The Living Christ is hence everywhere immortal! And wherever the Living Christ is; in the glory in heaven or in the believer in earth, He is what He is at every place and at all times, as He proclaims the Majesty of Himself in the following words: "I AM THAT I AM!" *Hear ye Him!* And thus the believer who has all this imputed to him as a free gift, who meets the divine conditions comprehended in the symbolism of baptism (that he must be dead and stay thus always), has it *all* for himself, which of course gives him his derivative immortality. And, in effect, this is exactly what II Timothy 1:9-11 (with which compare I Timothy 6:16) is saying.

Consequently, we find the Apostle Paul proclaiming in Romans 8:29: "For whom He did foreknow, He also did predestinate to be *conformed to the image of His Son,* that He might be the Firstborn among many brethren." Also he repeats the same thought of miraculous Begettal in Galatians 4:19, which expresses to those whom the Apostle calls his "little children" the one aim uppermost in his gospel ministry: "of whom [he states] I travail in birth again until *Christ be formed in you.*" And as already seen in Colossians 1:26, 27, in terms of Spiritual Biology, he emphazises the same concept and aim; namely, to present the mystery which he says is: "Christ in You, the Hope of Glory!"

A faint clue to the mystery of the Begettal, focussed in the foregoing as *the imaged Christ,* may be gathered from the simple illustration of our TV sets. In the field of television a central station or studio with broadcasting equipment and accompanying paraphernalia and facilities, supplies sufficient electrical energy (measured as a certain number of watts) which is then sent out (transmitted or radiated) through space in the form of invisible impulses and waves. These are in fact an emanation, continuation, extension, or extrusion of the original energy and, being thus of the same identity, can always be traced back to their source or point of departure.

This invisible energy, although all about us, is still something of which everyone is quite unaware until he flicks a switch or turns a knob in his home. While it is otherwise unperceived by any of the physical senses, it nevertheless manifests its presence through activating *only certain receivers* which have the necessary built-in adjustments and parts and are in turn correctly tuned to the same broadcast wave length or channel. *Presto!* the resulting activation at once produces (shall we say, begets?) an exact image or imprint of the things present at the point of origin. This, quite obviously, everyone concerned or interested can see and witness for himself.

The energy as it leaves the broadcast studio is invisible, yet the pervasive reality of its radiance is everywhere visibly present in the hundreds and thousands and even millions of home sets scattered over a wide area, *if they are properly attuned.* No one can realize through the sensory perceptions the reality of its invisible presence in the surrounding ether until it is seen with the naked eye in the pickup of the home set. Thus in every home the same exact image is reproduced, the same miraculous "begettal" takes place; everywhere the same magic prevails and everywhere it is actual and real. The broadcasting studio, while stationary in one location, is still everywhere as it diffuses itself in manifold images over the landscape.

And thus all the original things in the studio, together with the original atmosphere itself, can become "begotten again," or imaged, even at remote points. And if the ingenuity and spirit of man can do that much, and can do it so well with things finite and material, cannot the *Spirit of God* expressed in the *Living Christ,* through infinite power, and hence through the diffusion of His radiant energy, His cosmic or universal Presence, His indwelling immortal life and righteousness, do it even infinitely better?

The imaged Christ is hence no phantasy or myth of the human brain, nor yet a pipe dream or the guesswork and figment of the human imagination. The Presence of the vital Christ in reciprocal relationship to, and perfect union and coordination with, the believer is even more real, more potent, and on a firmer basis in every way, than TV. Consequently, the Begettal of the imaged Christ through believing in Him and in "the Power of His Resurrection" becomes an established verity and an indisputable reality. And every believer, moreover, has within himself the *witness* of this Begettal, which is the Witness of God, which is not dependent on outside corroboration or approval, the evidence being the *Divine Quickening* which invariably and infallibly follows.

23.   *The Imaged Christ a Literal New Creation*

The soul as the inner core or sheath (the nucleus which expresses the inward man, this being the psyche or ego) in the old or First Adam is quite as mysterious, inscrutable and elusive and quite as distinct as is the Spirit itself which divinely supersedes and replaces it and which expresses the inward man in the new or Second Adam, in terms of the *Imaged Christ*. One is as literal as the other and both are equally inexplicable in terms of human definition and comprehension. One thing both have in common, however, and that is the power of communication, as expressed through the medium of speech. Conversation, among other aspects, is the indelible hallmark of both soul and spirit. (Cf. Genesis 4:10 and Revelation 6:9-11.)

In scriptural usage, the soul is associated with the blood, the mind, and so with the excellency of knowledge, and is hence the medium of consciousness and sensation, and the focal seat of knowledge and intellect, passion and feeling, memory and imagination. The union of *Spirit and matter* produces soul—soul being intermediate between the two and subsequent to both. Thus, in relation to flesh, the soul is primarily focussed in the *blood.* (Cf. Genesis 9:4; Leviticus 17: 11, 14 and Deuteronomy 12:23.)

It is from this association that the name *Adam* itself is derived, which in the breakdown of its Hebrew etymology is *Aleph* ("first") plus *Dam* ("blood"), meaning *First Blood!* Called by the ancients "Divine Fire," the Spirit expresses the *primum mobile* (or First Cause and hence Ultimate Source) which kindles in flesh the vital spark of life, and without this Divine Essence, the body of man is just simply so much insensate matter—being just a clod of dirt. It is the Spirit Essence, namely, the Spirit of God, which sparks man into a condition of separate animated existence and is consequently the invisible force which awakens him into becoming *"a living soul!"*—Genesis 2:7.

Even so, we understand quite realistically the nature of the soul and the mystery of its workings through certain definite characteristics (or sensations) which become externally manifested and which establish the indisputable reality of its existence as the seat of personality consciousness. And likewise, using the same approach, we can understand the reality of the existence of the *new spirit* identity, the new seat of personality consciousness within the same Adamic framework, which comes into embryonic formation and development as a literal new creation in Christ Jesus, *the result of the New Begettal from above.* (Cf. Psalms 51: 10; Ephesians 4:24 and Colossians 3:10.) It, too, has its own set of distinctive characteristics which become externally manifested through flesh and blood and which exactly express the Imaged Christ as the newly begotten spirit or foetal entity—the "new soul," shall we say?

The personality in the old Adam manifests itself invariably through "the affections and lusts" inseparable from the body of flesh and blood (the framework) in which the soul resides—being the carnal sensations and instincts as these operate through the five senses in man—which they who have been begotten again, because "they are Christ's," have indeed crucified. As told in Jeremiah 17:9, the personality characteristics of the old Adamic soul establish its inherent and utter incorrigibility, which can be either dormant or active, latent or seething, quiescent or volcanic. Not even man himself—*any man*, that is—at his best can fathom the depths of his own iniquitous, treacherous, and depraved nature; nor yet its potentialities and possibilities, even when every prospect is pleasing and all is outwardly placid and unruffled. Hidden within the inner recesses of the old Adamic nature and lurking deep down beneath the surface of its pretended calm and goodwill, and perhaps even unsuspected, the sleeping furies lie, seemingly peaceful. But they are all ready to burst forth suddenly and malignantly, uproariously and intemperately, vengefully and viciously, at the slightest provocation, or without any pretext at all, depending on the excitement of the moment or the occasion and circumstances of its innate turmoil and wrath. At this lamentable juncture, self-righteous man on the defensive brazenly and insolently attempts to justify himself in the eyes of other humans who are every whit as mortal and frail and culpable as he, all being the creatures of dust and all tarred with the same brush. Indeed, he attempts to rationalize and excuse his misdeeds generally and his inhumanity particularly through resorting to a fantastic stratagem which in itself is a masterpiece of subterfuge and self-deceit, and which takes the form of appealing to other men who are just like himself; all of which winds up a vicious circle and all of which therefore proves quite futile, hopeless, and unavailing in the eyes of God. Man doesn't really know himself, *but God does!*

"As it is written, *there is none righteous, no, not one!* there is none that seeketh after God. They are all gone out of the way, they are together become unprofitable; *there is none that doeth good, no, not one!* Their throat is an open sepulcher; with their tongues they have used deceit; the poison of asps is under their lips: whose mouth is full of cursing and bitterness: their feet are swift to shed blood: de-

struction and misery are in their ways: and the way of peace
have they not known: there is no fear of God before their
eyes. . . . *For all have sinned and come short of the glory
of God.*"—Romans 3:10-23.

And this is because the divine standards pertaining to
righteousness and holiness are so transcendently unap-
proachable and so far beyond the reach and attainment of
the natural Adamic man that a whole new creation, combining a whole new order of things, becomes absolutely necessary. Out with the old, in with the new—that is distinctly the
message conveyed in the Word found in II Corinthians 5:17!
In this connection, the prophet Habakkuk tells us that the
mighty God, in the matchless character and splendor of His
Divinity and His supernal righteousness and holiness, is of
such "purer eyes than to behold evil and look on iniquity"
with even the least degree of allowance.—Habakkuk 1:13.

Indeed, many Christians—probably the greater number
of them—with smug complacency and undisguised indiffer-
ence get no further in their approach to this crucial issue
than to blame the Devil personally as being the immediate
and exciting cause of all that is base and bestial, criminal
and cruel, violent and vicious, inhuman and infernal in man:
even, for that matter, blaming Satan himself for some of
their own carnal perversities, monstrous excesses, and truly
fiendish and hellish misdeeds in the realm of human rela-
tions. And from there, in their blindness and stupidity, said
Christians go on to extol the alleged virtues of civilization as
the be-all and end-all of salvation and the cure-all for the
world's ills. In their loose thinking, they pretend that the
symbols of materialism—money, education, culture and power—which they equate with moral development and godly
uplift, somehow make for progress and reform and even
regeneration. Such Christians fail to recognize that what the
world stands mostly in need of, including their own dear

selves, is not so much moral reformation as it is *spiritual transformation*. And they forget, of course, that it is also written, "Vengeance is Mine, I will repay, saith the LORD," —which especially applies to the Hereafter. In this connection, the Divine vengeance will certainly be poured out and heaped upon all those guilty of monstrous inhumanity together with all forms of evildoing, including the indignities and excesses committed upon the persons of other humans created in the image of the same Maker and the same Redeemer. Alas and alack, "it is a fearful thing to fall into the hands of the Living God."—Hebrews 10:31.

In their spiritual obtuseness and bankruptcy, many there are who mistakenly regard education (including the arts and sciences and the humanities) and religion so-called (which they superficially exemplify), together with various cultural and civic activities, as the fount of every blessing. And they rely upon same in ever increasing prescription and extension as the veritable shoe-straps by which alone man can be saved and lift himself into the pearly gates. Assessing this poignant situation in terms of a duped world, one of God's studious and approved workmen[2] with penetrating insight rightly observes:

> "It is only when we accept fully the testimony of God concerning the world that we come to know that, just as in the natural man dwelleth no good thing, but that he is irretrievably corrupt; so likewise in the world there are no good works, but on the contrary, 'the works thereof are evil'; and that, in fact, its best works are its worst. Just as in the natural man, there is nothing capable of development by culture, reform, or moral training (*which are the worst enemies of regeneration*) to render him meet for the presence of God; so likewise there is no germ or principle of good in the world capable of development under the influence of culture, education, religion, etc. (*which are the most potent*

---

[2] Philip Mauro in *Man's Day*, pp. 158, 159, as quoted in *The Faith Magazine* (England), January-February, 1927.

enemy of the personal return of Christ[3]), to render it fit for the presence of God."

In the natural or "soulish" man, we are therefore all of us unreconstructed rebels and miscreants, whether we know it or not, or whether we even like it or not. Miserable creatures of dust we all are, saturated with perfidy and iniquity, brimming up to our eyes with deceit and guile and hate, and exuding out of both ears everything festering, corrupt, perverse and vile, and everything malodorous, obnoxious, and contemptible. The old Adamic man, clothed in the habiliments of his own self-esteem and self-righteousness, is a stench in God's nostrils. Accordingly, it is also written: "The heart is deceitful above all things, and desperately wicked: *who can know it?*" (Cp. John 2:24, 25) John 2:24, 25.

On the other hand, the seat of personality in the Second Adam (which represents the divine beginning—the bedrock and foundation—of the new creation in Christ Jesus, expressed as the Begettal) manifests itself through the complete regeneration which now occurs *deep down inside* (in the inward parts, corresponding to the believer's womb), mysterious, unfathomable, and inexplicable as this too is. So that (Ephesians 4:22-24) "concerning the former conversation the old man, which is corrupt according to the deceitful lusts, is put off; the spirit of the mind is renewed; and the *new man* which after God is *created* in righteousness and true holiness becomes put on instead." Also (Philippians 3: 20, 21) the "conversation is in heaven, whence also we look for the Saviour, the LORD JESUS CHRIST: who shall change our vile body, that it may be fashioned like unto His glorious body, according to the working whereby He is able to subdue all things unto Himself."

Hence (Romans 12:2), it is "by the renewing of the

---

[3] In our presentation of *The New Birth,* the personal return of Christ expresses itself literally in terms of His Personal Indwelling, as manifested through "the Power of His Resurrection."

mind" that the believer finds himself "*transformed;*" and finding himself "acceptable and perfect" in this transcendent divine sense, he is accounted worthy, which is the "will of God." And thus he fulfills the state of grace alluded to in the Sermon on the Mount, which is seen in the royal command: "*Be ye therefore perfect, even as your Father which is in heaven is perfect.*"—Matthew 5:48. The focus of his interest and conversation being put in reverse gear, the believer accordingly gives heed to the admonition found in Colossians 3:1-3: "If ye then be risen with Christ [in other words, if ye be *begotten again*], seek those things which are above [celestial], where Christ sitteth on the right hand of God. Set your affections on things above, not on things on the earth. *For ye are dead, and your life is hid with Christ in God.*"

The Imaged Christ, the result of the Divine Begettal, becomes the personality expression of the inwardly regenerated man; and, as such, is therefore the embryonic *Seed* or "Christ in You, the Hope of Glory." Consequently, it manifests itself in the believer through the changed emphasis, pitch, and tone of his conversation, as seen in the reversal of its direction. Heretofore carnal, it is now *renewed* and hence completely transformed and made spiritual.

His newly begotten *spirit,* no longer employed in filthy and unprofitable conversation reflecting a heart that is impure and insincere, one that is "deceitful above all things and desperately wicked," engages itself in spiritual exercises. That is to say, the New Man is occupied in spiritual meditation and contemplation, piety and positive living, constructive thoughts, attitudes and postures (Philippians 4:8), in devotion to the principles of true Christian charity and magnanimity (I Corinthians 13); and in the cultivation of "the fruits of the Spirit" (Galatians 5:22, 23),—which all increase to "righteousness and true holiness." The carnal mind inseparably belonging to the soulish natural man is now superseded, thanks to the Divine Love and Mercy expressed through the Divine Begettal, which brings this miracle of grace to pass, and henceforth, being a New Creature in

Christ Jesus, the believer's "conversation is in heaven."

Is this not in itself the ineluctable evidence of the *New Soul's* divinity? Is this not *per se* "the Witness of God" mentioned in I John 5:9-12 and expressed as the Divine Quickening in one's own mortal being? Does it not infallibly verify the *New Soul's* celestial origin and immortal inheritance, as connected up to its own divine identity expressed in the Imaged Christ, its celestial Source? And does this not, by that very token, attest the existence and reality of the *New Soul* in the Imaged Christ as *a literal New Creation,* the focus indeed of the believer's *other self,* whose own identity thus coincides with the identity of the risen, ascended, and glorified Christ no less, expressing Himself in the selfsame terms of His Indwelling Presence?

Verily, "he that believeth on the Son of God hath 'the Witness' in himself: *he that believeth not God hath made Him a liar,* because he believeth not the record that God gave of His Son!"

24. The Seed of the Begettal—the Word of Faith

At the very outset of this topical consideration, we have the specific declaration from Paul that it was the Gospel which he used in his Gentile ministry to beget his little ones in Christ Jesus. In Galatians 4:19, we find him speaking to "my little children of whom I travail in birth until *Christ be formed in you,*" and further telling us in I Corinthians 4:15: "for in Christ Jesus I have begotten you *through the Gospel.*"

Likewise the Apostle James is emphatic about the matter, declaring "of His own will begat He us with *the Word of truth,* that we should be a kind of firstfruits of His creatures."—James 1:18. James is harking to his own definite identification with the Pentecostal Firstfruits of the Apostolic Era and the concomitant sealing out of the twelve Hebrew tribes which went along with this, to which he is here also adding his personal witness, and in which he was conscious of having a secure place in the celestial heritage allotted to the Headship of Christ. (Cf. Romans 8:19-23 and I Corinthians 15:20-23.)

To the foregoing, Peter, too, states: "Being begotten again not of corruptible seed but of incorruptible [seed], *by the Word of God*, which liveth and abideth for the eons." And for the benefit of those not quite comprehending what he means, Peter has already left no doubt that it is *"by the Resurrection of Jesus Christ from the dead"* we are thus *"begotten again unto a lively hope."*—I Peter 1:3, 23. Of course Peter is saying, as Paul has said, there is "Power in His Resurrection" *to beget and save!*

The foregoing all adds up to this: that the Gospel is *good news!* That it is the good news of "salvation to everyone that believeth," which expresses "the Power of God" through the Resurrection of Christ Jesus the Lord, and which thus spells out the resultant Begettal and the believer's justification by faith. In turn, the good news becomes literally expressed in terms of the following substitute arrangement, on the basis of even exchange, but nevertheless a one-sided, unfair, and wholly undeserved exchange. Howbeit since it is satisfactory to the divine party, it should at once be acceptable to the human party.

Hence, as provided in the good news, God's unique arrangement for the redemption of mankind involves the following, bestowed as a free divine gift and constituting the heart of His Gospel to humanity. The Divine Life itself is substituted for the believer's sinful life; the Divine Righteousness itself is substituted for the believer's unrighteousness; the Divine Immortality itself is substituted for the believer's mortality; the Divine Light itself is substituted for the believer's darkness and blindess; the Divine Illumination itself is substituted for the believer's misunderstanding. This gracious gift further includes the following *literal* inheritance and benefits: a brand-new spirit-soul begotten into the believer's present Adamic carcass and fleshly identity, plus a brand-new body from the Father's heavenly storehouse, with which he is "born" at the dissolution of his

Adamic identity; both the spirit-soul and the body being
of divine origin and constituting the formation and manifestation of the Celestial New Creature in Christ Jesus.
(Cf. Isaiah 64:6; 1:18 and 55:1. Also Cp. 6:5-7.)

25. The Heart of the Faith-Gospel

In simplest form, the Word of Faith which is the seed
of the Begettal is the Gospel of salvation and life, as divinely proclaimed in John 3:16: "For God so loved the
world that He gave His only begotten Son, that whosoever
believeth in Him should not perish, but have eonian life."
(That is to say, *life in the eons* starting with the present
eon allotted to the nations, or Gentiles. See Topic No. 12
for further elucidation of this important subject.)

The importance of this glorious proclamation to humanity everywhere and throughout all time, comprehending the
Faith Gospel divinely commissioned to be published in all
the inhabited world to *all nations,* is elsewhere emphasized
in such passages as the following which represent the key-
stone and heart of that Gospel.

John 1:12, 13:   "But as many as received Him, to them
gave He power [through His Resurrection, hence through
the correlative divine processes in the *New Birth*] to become
the sons of God, even to them that believe in His Name:
which were begotten [Gr.], not of blood, nor of the will of
the flesh, nor of the will of man, but of God."

James 1:18: "Of His own will begat He us with the Word
of truth . . ."

I John 5:11-13:   "And this is the record, that God hath
given to us eonian life, and this life is in His Son. *He that
hath the Son hath life; and he that hath not the Son of God
hath not life.* These things have I written unto you that believe on the Name of the Son of God; that ye may know
that ye have eonian life, and that ye may believe on the
Name of the Son of God."

Acts 4:12: Niether is there salvation in any other: for there is none other Name under heaven given among men whereby we must be saved."

John 5:24: "Verily, verily, I say unto you, He that heareth My Word, and believeth on Him that sent Me, hath eonian life, and shall not come into condemnation; *but is passed from death unto life.*"

John 11:25-27: "Jesus said unto Martha, I am the Resurrection and the Life: he that believeth in Me, though he were dead, yet shall he live: *and whosoever liveth and believeth in Me shall never die.* Believeth thou this? She saith unto Him, Yea, Lord: I believe that Thou are the Christ, the Son of God, which should come into the world."

Revelation 1:18: "I am He that liveth and was dead; and behold, I am alive forever more [Gr. to the ages of the ages], Amen; and have the keys of hell [the grave] and of death."

Matthew 16:15-18: "He saith unto His disciples, But whom say ye that I am? And Simon Peter answered and said, *Thou art the Christ, the Son of the Living God!* And Jesus answered and said unto him, Blessed art thou, Simon Barjona: for flesh and blood hath not revealed it unto thee, but My Father which is in heaven. And I say unto thee, That thou art Peter, and *upon this Rock* [meaning *the Rock of Peter's confession* preceding, not by any chance Peter the man himself!] I will build My Church [the Celestial Body of Christ itself, composed of those spirit-souls gone into glory at death and therefore "born" into the Kingdom of God]; and the gates of hell [the Grave and hence Death itself] shall not prevail against it."

Philippians 3:8-11: "Yea, doubtless, and I count all things but loss for the excellency of the knowledge of CHRIST JESUS my Lord: for whom I have suffered the loss of all things, and do count them but dung, that I may win Christ, and be found in Him, not having mine own righteousness which is of the law [the *deeds* of the law, that is], *but that which is through the faith of Christ, the Righteousness which is of God by Faith* [hence imputed and assigned Righteousness]: that I may know Him, and THE POWER OF HIS RESURRECTION, and the fellowship of His sufferings, being made conformable unto His death; if by any means I might attain unto the resurrection of the dead [the *exanastasis* or out-resurrection]."

II Timothy 1:8-11: "But be thou partaker of the afflictions of the Gospel according to *the Power of God* [same expressing the Power of the Resurrection]: who hath saved us, and called us with an holy calling, not according to our works, but according to His own purpose and grace, which was given us in Christ Jesus before the world began. But is now made manifest by the appearing of our Saviour Jesus Christ, *who hath abolished death* [for the believer] *and hath brought life and immortality to light through the Gospel* [for the believer]: whereunto I am appointed a preacher, and an apostle, and a teacher of the Gentiles [Gr. nations]."

Matthew 28:18-20: "And Jesus came and spake unto His disciples, saying, all Power [namely, as in Romans 1:4, through His Resurrection] is given unto Me in heaven, and in earth. Go ye therefore and teach [disciple] ALL NATIONS, *baptizing* them [through the burial rite which in its usage and interpretation expresses *immersion*] into THE NAME of the Father [LORD] and of the Son [JESUS] and of the Holy Spirit [CHRIST]."

The key passages above relating to the New Birth (to which many others of like tenor and substance, and just as pertinent and lucid, could be added) comprehend and confirm the heart of the Faith-Gospel to humanity, which is the seed of the Begettal. And even as with Martha to whom the Name of the Resurrection identity (*Christ, the Son of the Living God!*) was patently revealed, and with Peter to whom likewise flesh and blood did not reveal it, and with Paul who came to *know* its vital essence and meaning, all we have to do, on our part, is just simply to believe in the Christ of the Ascended Glory, THE LIVING CHRIST HIM-SELF, and in "the Power of His Resurrection": and forthwith the miracle of Begettal will take place and we shall be "begotten again" and "found with child of the Holy Spirit," and verily created anew.

Yea, verily, we shall be saved to dwell together with Him in celestial places, and we shall begin, *even as of here and now,* the enjoyment of the more abundant life which in its promise of greater and better things, summed up as a new order of things, and in the meaning and dimensions of its infinite profusion and its uninterrupted continuity and splendor beyond death and the grave, spells IMMORTAL-ITY!

26. *The Seed as Living Spiritual Water*

At this juncture we wish to make it unmistakably clear that apart from and without the seed of the Living Word of faith implanted in the womb of the believer's heart, thus to fecundate the ovaries thereof, there can be no Begettal at all of the Imaged Christ. Distributed and disseminated as this has to be by the preaching and hearing of the Gospel of salvation and life, the seminal seed of the Word as the vitalizing principle or sperm comes into the believer's inward parts through the use of a divine euphemism which introduces it as *living Spiritual Water,* therein to fecundate and generate the invisible formation which is "Christ in you" —henceforth the New Creation which is the believer's other self. (Cf. John 3:5; 7:38, 39 and 15:33 with Ephesians 5:26, where Paul uses the same figure of speech to express "the washing of *water* by the Word.")

Thus the inward spirit (the new soul), created anew in Christ Jesus, comes alive through the vitalizing "Power of His Resurrection" in the inflow of *the Spirit's Water* which first penetrates and then begets. And in this state of vital Christian experience which is its climactic moment of divine ecstasy (biologically expressed in the orgasm), the believer finds himself daily "renewed in the spirit of his mind," due to the fact that he has "put on the new man which after God is *created* in righteousness and true holiness." To put it another way, he has been *begotten again!* (Ephesians 4:23, 24; 2:10 and Colossians 3:10 and II Corinthians 4:16.)

Paul explains the romancing and copulation of the believer together with the intromission of the Divine Seed as follows: "So then faith cometh by hearing, and hearing by the Word of God." He also explains:

> "The Word is nigh thee, even in thy mouth, and in thy heart; that is, *the Word of Faith*, which we preach: that if thou shalt confess with thy mouth the LORD JESUS, *and shalt believe in thine heart that God hath raised Him from the dead, thou shalt be saved.* For with the heart man believeth unto righteousness, and with the mouth confession is made unto salvation. For the Scripture saith, Whosoever believeth on Him shall not be ashamed."—Romans 10:8-17.

Which is of course what Peter means when he states: "Being *begotten again*, not of corruptible seed [fleshly semen], but of incorruptible Seed [Spiritual Water, which is to say,] *by the Word of God*, which liveth and abideth for the eons."

Let us make no mistake—let us make it crystal clear! The foetal or Imaged Christ thus inwardly generated and formed (in short, begotten!) by the invisible sperm in the Word of Faith is one and the same in literal organic identity and form, in literal Spirit essence and content, and hence in literal being and vital unity, with the Cosmic Christ which it represents—the former expressed as the Indwelling of His Presence within the believer, the latter as His universal Spirit or Essence outside the believer "in which we live, move, and have our being": and both together constituting the indivisible organic whole which is THE BODY OF CHRIST.

Perhaps we can now understand the underlying meaning

of Christ being in us as well as our being in Christ. And, celestially considered, perhaps we can now sense the sort of reciprocal relationship inherent in our being in organic union and identity with Him. There is of course deep spiritual significance in both aspects. As shown in John 14:26; 15:26; 16:13-19; Acts 1:8; 2:1-4, the Living Christ is seen as THE HOLY SPIRIT (the *to Pneuma to Hagion,* in the Gr. with the article), also as the *Paraclete,* the Comforter and Advocate. In Ephesians 4:10 and Revelation 5:6, He is seen as the Universal or Cosmic Spirit. In John 15: 1-8, He is the Indwelling Presence under the figure of the true Vine and its branches, representing the single organic identity and vital union between the Christ of the Ascended Glory and the believer which expresses *"Ye in Me and I in you!"*

Through impregnation with the seminal seed of the Living Word, the Cosmic or Universal Christ comes into the believer's heart as the vital principle which expresses the Indwelling Christ. The result of this entrance—the penetration—is the Imaged Christ *in utero,* begotten there by THE SPIRIT'S seminal Water. The Christ thus formed within is one and the same with the Universal Christ without, being a portion of the same radiant Energy and Fire, the same Universal Essence, the same Omnipresence, and the same Celestial Identity. Reduced to its lowest divine denominator which is the embryonic Christ, the Living Christ within is now the believer's other self through operation of justification by faith. Hence, through divine imputation and assignment, the Life and Righteousness of the One becomes the undying and indefeasible possession of the other. In fact, all the perquisites, attributes and rights inherent in the One become inherited by the other, and it is thus the believer derives and acquires the Life, the Righteousness, and the Immortality of the Son of God. It is thus that the believer claims all these for himself, which he henceforth has the right to call his very own. A simple matter of divine bookkeeping, this being the crux of the doctrine of justification by faith! (Cp. Romans 6:9.)

The resultant infusion and infilling of the divine life is the genesis forthwith of the invisible new identity which is subsequently to emerge at its New Birth, with "the manifestation of the sons of God." It is then with the death of the old Adamic carcass, as it passes through the chrysalis stage which witnesses the mortification and corruption of its flesh and blood and bones, that the believer is "born" into his eonian inheritance and becomes a manifested son of God. It is then in the lightning quick metamorphosis which takes place at the very instant of mortal dissolution that he acquires his status in celestial glory as a glorified and redeemed inhabitant of the Kingdom of God.

The Apostle Paul writes: "Now this I say, brethren, that flesh and blood cannot inherit the Kingdom of God; neither doth corruption inherit incorruption"; and further declares "there is a natural body and there is a spiritual body," one being as *literal* as the other and both thus divinely appropriate to the medium in which each can exist and function best.—II Corinthians 15:42-50. This of course agrees with what was previously uttered by the Master Himself, found recorded in John 3:3, 5: "Verily, verily, I say unto thee, Except a man be begotten again *of Water and the Spirit* [meaning THE SPIRIT'S own seminal Water, which thus becomes *Living Spiritual Water*], he cannot see nor can he enter into the Kingdom of God."

27. The "Gumnon-Kokkon" in I Corinthians 15:36, 37

Before going into our topical follow-up on the Divine Quickening (see Topic No. 29), we wish at this point to consider parenthetically a topic connected with the believer's metamorphosis, or evolution, into a *manifested son of God,* which as just seen is also very much a part of the Spiritual Biology of the New Birth. As used by the Apostle Paul in I Corinthians 15:37, the Greek *gumnon-kokkon* (translated "bare grain" or "naked seed," and as such the naked or unclothed "cocoon") specifically focusses the new celestial identity which comes into being with the mortal death of the believer. The Greek word *kokkon* suggests our English "cocoon," consequently referring to the evolutionary changes which take place in the life cycle of the butterfly and other winged insects. In terms of plain everyday natural biology, the word *cocoon* leaves no room for misunderstanding and at once gives us an immediate clue to its correct divine meaning.

The allusion to "wheat" in verse 37 directly places our topical discussion in the field of plant life. However, this fact *per se* does not alter the vitality of our reasoning along biological lines, which necessarily deal with both animal and plant growth. The same factual presentation is involved and the same valid inferences are to be drawn in the one instance as in the other. The *germ* in the wheat which is its core—the cotyledon—is surrounded by a hull or husk, which in turn is analogous to a cocoon. It is this outer wheat shell, jacket, or carcass which must first die in order that the wheat germ within it might become *quickened!* The approach and the reasoning are the same in both cases.

From the encyclopedias we learn that "Cocoon is the name given to the web, ball, or silky case spun by the caterpillar to protect itself before passing into the chrysalis or torpid state," the latter of course being "the form which butterflies, moths, flies, and other insects assume when they change from the larva or caterpillar state and before they arrive at their winged or perfect state." The chrysalis is hence "the torpid stage of passive development between the larva form (caterpillar) and subsequent transformation form (butterfly, etc.)."

In its metamorphosis from caterpillar to butterfly, the inner core or nucleus which is the expression of its larva form must first *die* before it can be revitalized into the winged form, this being the intermediate condition or chrysalis stage of the lowly caterpillar before it changes into the butterfly form of its existence. As soon as it emerges from the torpid stage (the chrysalis), to leave the casing or shell of its previous habitation behind for keeps, the butterfly which is the same in identity with the caterpillar, being thus "born" into its new existence and form, at once wings its way upward into the blue empyrean, flitting hither and yon and being no longer circumscribed with the limitations of its lowly ugly past, its repulsive worm-form, its ungainly and clumsy crawl, and its other limitations.

Even thus, through mighty invisible divine power which expresses "the Power of His Resurrection," "the soul that on Jesus rests" undergoes a similar metamorphosis (which is its spiritual evolution and transformation embracing the period of its gestation) when it too is "born," thus taking it out of its fleshly sinful habitation with all its hideous and repulsive past, the features, traits, and propensities of its previous Adamic existence. And at the moment when it leaves all this behind, to emerge from its ugly low-life chrysalis into the sunlit "manifestation of the sons of God," that soul at once emerges into literal "newness of life" to ascend to realms of immortal glory and supernal bliss, being indeed "a new creature in Christ Jesus" fit for celestial habitation. And thus fitted for the company of angels, the four Zoa and twenty-four Presbyters, together with the Lamb Himself, it is henceforth overclothed with its new mansion from heaven, when it is no longer circumscribed or encumbered with the previous limitations inherent to its Adamic carcass, its fleshly blood heritage and its earthly mode of existence,— which is further connected to its over-all limitations in time and space and matter *as well as sin.* (Cf. II Corinthians 5: 1-4 and John 14:1-4.)

To those who in their blinded hostility question this invisible phenomenon and who thus question its consummation as a literal divine reality, which is indeed beyond all sense and sight and sound, Paul replies: "Thou fool, that which thou sowest is not quickened, *except it die!*"—I Corinthians 15:36. The external casing or shell of the old Adamic form which encases the chrysalis or begotten identity of the believer must slough off and die, in order for the divinely generated New Creature within to be *"made perfect"* and thus to come alive into the inheritance of its glorious body from heaven, which (verse 38) it pleaseth God to give.

Putting it another way, the encased identity (or chrysalis) around which the web, ball, or silky case constituting the cocoon is spun must become "bare or naked," entirely bereft of its old casing or outer shell, before it can emerge into the sunlight of a new existence and so enter into the Kingdom of God. And this is what the figurative *gumnonkokkon* precisely expresses, in terms of Spiritual Biology. The phenomenon of mortal death is the phenomenon which, *for the believer* (not the unbeliever), releases his new-born spirit entity (the chrysalis) from its outer Adamic casing (the cocoon),—which is *"Christ in you!" formed at the Begettal.* It is hence the "open sesame" and the inviting gateway to immortality and celestial glory which the believer acquires in Him, from Him, and through Him. *It is a gift!*

And thus the abundant Life hidden with Christ in glory becomes unfolded in all its fullness and wideness and depth in the New Birth of the believer, which takes the form of his new celestial existence "in the midst of the Paradise of God" and which thereby "translates him into the Kingdom of His dear Son"—the Celestial BODY OF CHRIST.—Revelation 2:7 and Colossians 1:13.

Thanks to the poet who caught the heavenly vision of "Life Only in Christ Jesus" which, in the rapture of his glowing tribute to the beauty of holiness in the sweetness of prayer, he lyrically expresses for us in the well-known verses of song:

> "Sweet hour of prayer, sweet hour of prayer,
> May I thy consolation share,
> Till from Mount Pisgah's lofty height,
> I view my home, and take my flight.

> "This robe of flesh I'll drop and rise
> To seize the everlasting prize;
> And shout, while passing through the air,
> Farewell, farewell, sweet hour of prayer."

28. *The Mystery of the Hereafter*

"But as it is written, Eye hath not seen, nor ear heard, neither have entered into the heart of man, the things which God hath prepared for them that love Him."—I Corinthians 2:9.

Without a doubt, the foregoing includes—within the scope of the divine surprises which, as stated, are far and away beyond the fondest dreams, imaginations, hopes, and expectations of the human soul—the heavenly mansions (or redemption bodies) which are for celestial habitation. In the Hereafter immediately following the dissolution of the Adamic "cocoon," new bodies are waiting for those who love God supremely *"with all their heart and with all their soul and with all their mind and with all their strength."* These are they who in their heart, and in the demonstration of their life, have the same genuine love for their neighbor as they have for themselves, and who have thereby been "begotten again," accordingly to become "translated into the Kingdom of His dear Son," which is THE BODY OF CHRIST!—Mark 12:30, 31; Colossians 1:13.

Unfortunately, many of us are so incurably unbelieving with respect to these vital matters as not to be able to conceive (let alone concede!) the *reality* of anything happening or existing that is outside the boundaries of mortal sense and sight and sound. Unless it can happen according to our preconceptions or our desires and unless it is scientifically demonstrable, we demur, we doubt, we scoff, we deny. But not so, says Paul in I Corinthians 2:14, declaring "the natural man cannot receive the things of the Spirit of God, which are only foolishness to him, because they are *spiritually discerned.*"

Wisely has one writer said: "In our being and thinking we are so inherently terrestrial that it seems almost impossible for us to conceive being transported into the realms of space away from the earth." He might have added that he did not have in mind space ships, rockets, turbojets, satellite launchings, or any such machines. True reality and existence lie in the unseen, the intangible, and the impalpable; and only the eye of faith can perceive it. Only faith can grasp the reality of the existence that is beyond soulish description or attainment, the reality that is also beyond scientific demonstration, beyond the laboratory, and even beyond extra sensory perception.

Let us then have simple *Christian* faith. In more meaningful and explicit language, let us have *"the Faith of Jesus!"* For therein, indeed, lies the seed of our begettal—the Spiritual Water which begets us anew in Christ Jesus, thus to enable us to dwell together with Him and to enjoy "all spiritual blessings in heavenly places in Christ." (Revelation 14:12 and Ephesians 1:3.)

> Hebrews 11:1: "Now faith is the *substance* of things hoped for [hence the reality of things also to be waited for], the *evidence* of things not seen [likewise substantiating the reality of the invisible]."
>
> II Corinthians 4:18: "While we look not at the things which are seen [hence demonstrable], but at things which are not seen [hence not being subject to demonstration]: for the things which are seen are *temporal* [i.e., being in time, temporary and fugitive, and thus ephemeral; hence they soon vanish away, being like a vapor]; but the things which are not seen are eonian."

The life which the believer has in the Son, exactly because it is invisible, is eonian life, which makes it enduring, and is hence the only true reality as far as the Hereafter is concerned. The believer therefore knows he can depend on the reality of his eonian life in the Hereafter, because he has it here and now, having the Son in him. And because the Son's Life is inherently immortal, he knows he has this, too, in a derived sense. And in this all-important sense, he knows it is abundant and constant, and that he will have it to enjoy in the infinite Hereafter, because "He is *faithful* that promised, who also will do it," which divinely takes care of any mystery attaching to the Hereafter. (Hebrews

10: 23; I Thessalonians 5:24 and Revelation 19:11.)

Moreover, because the believer has the infallible "Witness of God" in him, which expresses the begettal of his *new soul,* he knows he can safely and sweetly rest in the blessed assurance, even as "the Scripture saith, *Whosoever believeth on Him shall not be ashamed!"*—Romans 10:11.

29. Follow-up—the Divine Quickening

Picking up the thread of our previous discussion under Topic No. 26 relative to the seminal inflow of Living Spiritual Water, we come now to the crux of the exposition embracing our third thematic dimension. The fact of conception, actually the direct outcome and literal fruit of the begettal, becomes infallibly manifested to the believer himself, and to no one else immediately or directly, in the *divine quickening* which soon follows the event, finding its exact counterpart in the similar sequences and experience of natural birth as we perceive this in fleshly generation.

Quickening is an undeniable personal experience, with its own characteristic manifestations, that only scoffers and fools would dare to decry, laugh or poke fun at. It is a vital manifestation of life generated—a new life begun. It is accompanied, moreover, by its own complex of associated sensations and reactions which the newly conceived infant just beginning to grow, though as yet unborn, itself produces, and is hence not dependent on any other person's witness or testimony to validate it or otherwise prove that it is vital and real.

The divine quickening is accordingly God's own heavenly manifestation and direct revelation of His personal abiding and His Own Presence within, which raises the believer to the level of a celestial. It is hence the infallible divine witness to the believer that he is begotten again: that he indeed has the personal infilling and indwelling of *the Holy Spirit*—the Vital Christ Himself—through whom exactly he becomes begotten. (Cf. I John 5:4-12.) In its infinite aspects and spiritual meaning, the divine quickening is comparable to the small boy flying a kite. At times he has to

fly it blind. And although in the distant reaches of its ma-
neuverings his kite may be out of sight up yonder, yet he
knows it is there from the tug and haul and pull on the
string. And so with the believer who, to use a quite apt
simile, finds himself in "the Way," knowing because of
certain inner signals which to him are unique and distin-
guishable and which he considers infallible, that he has
been truly begotten again! And continuing the force of the
simile, the believer can now begin *to expect,* knowing that
the certainty of his delivery at the New Birth has the same
infallible witness behind it and that the latter will come
duly.

Apropos of this topic, the Apostle Peter in quite explicit fashion explains the mystery of how the believer's other
self, as expressed in the Imaged Christ, is begotten. The end
result of this Begettal in divine terms being the invisible but
quite literal formation which is "Christ in you, the *Hope* of
glory!" It is begotten, not of fleshly semen which is corruptible, but by the Spirit's own seminal inflow of Water which
is incorruptible.—I Peter 1:23. Previously alluding to the
mystery of this unseen but vital formation within the believer, Peter in verse 3 of the same chapter calls attention to the
quickening which in every case follows the New Begettal,
even as it does in the natural, saying: "Blessed be the God
and Father of our LORD JESUS CHRIST, which according to His abundant mercy hath begotten us again unto *a
lively Hope* by the Resurrection [Power] of Jesus Christ
from the dead."

Peter is of course defining the same aftermath of the
Begettal which Paul in Colossians 1:27 expresses as "the
HOPE of glory." Peter, however, adds another facet to the
same idea of expectation, calling it "a *lively* hope!" By such
emphasis and distinction, Peter is calling attention to the
follow-up in the pre-natal state expressed in the quickening.
And as registered in the attendant circumstances of natural
pregnancy, this is subjectively experienced, as a vigorously
quivering movement of the living foetus in the womb which
can be both felt and seen. thus announcing its existence

and presence. As those in "the family way" all know, the experience is that of an intermittent palpitating or pulsating movement—a sort of knock-knock-at-the-door felt as a thumping of drumbeats,—being an altogether *lively* sensation which proclaims the fact of conception and generated life within; which indeed proclaims the existence and growth of the infant yet unborn and as yet invisible.

The same thing takes place within the inward parts of every true believer, which is reflected in the selfsame personal experience of an altogether glorious feeling in the awareness and sensitivity of a new life within, combined with a quite *lively* sensation which witnesses to the fact of his Begettal and which verily proclaims "The Witness of God" in him. The Radiant Fire of the Indwelling Presence having seized and overpowered him and lit him up, he in turn cannot let go of its fire nor can he snuff out the unquenchable burning of its inner flame, nor still yet can he suppress its knowledge and the telling and living of it.

Through "the Power of His Resurrection," the believer feels all this and more. He finds himself possessed and seized of a veritable "live wire" in his *new soul!* And thus is begotten the foetal or embryonic "Christ in you, *the HOPE of glory,*" the witness of which is always *itself!* In process of time and because of development and growth *in utero,* this initial "hope" at the conception of the believer further expresses itself in biological sequence as "*a lively hope*"—the infallible and continuing witness of the divine quickening.

In I John 5:7, 8, the Apostle John mentions that "there are three that bear record: ... The Spirit, and the Water, and the Blood: and these three agree in one."[4] He further adds in verses 9-12:

---

[4] *The Companion Bible* in its notes on verses 7 and 8 alerts us to the following: "The Texts read, 'the Spirit, and the water', & omitting all the words from 'in heaven' (v. 7) to 'in earth' (v. 8) inclusive. The words are not found in any Gr. ms. before the sixteenth century. They were first seen in the margin of some Latin copies. Thence they have crept into the [A.V.] text."

"If we receive the witness of men [which we have in the natural counterpart of gestation, which expresses the pre-natal state in the biological development of the foetus], the Witness of God is greater [even in the spiritual counterpart of gestation]: for *this* is the Witness of God which He hath testified of His Son [hence as follows]: *He that believeth on the Son of God hath the Witness in himself!* he that believeth not God hath made Him A LIAR; because he believeth not the record that God gave of His Son. *And this is the record*: that God hath given to us eonian [by virtue of which it becomes immortal!] life, *and this Life is in His Son. He that hath the Son hath life* [namely, His Life!]: and he that hath not the Son of God hath not life."

In other words, John is telling us that the Witness of Life is life itself, and life is of course never static, always expressing itself dynamically. Life that is life is constantly proliferating itself—begetting, growing, reproducing, and multiplying itself. The man who has the Life of the Son of God begotten into him (and this is the occasion of John's emphasis in the foregoing verses) has therefore the threefold "Witness of God in himself." As in earthly quickening, the divine quickening consequently comes into forceful play and dynamic activity with its own vital and compelling witness, thereby to announce the *Living Indwelling Presence* now in the form of the foetal Christ. Again as in mortal quickening, the Divine Witness is threefold, in that: 1) the begotten foetus which expresses the Life of the Son of God is literally in the believer *in utero*, thereby proclaiming the fact of his conception with child; "Christ in You!" being the living incarnation of *"the Lord Himself who is that Spirit"* (cf. II Corinthians 3:17) and hence being the infallible expression and witness of His own indwelling; 2) it is the Spirit's own seminal *Water of Life* which, with the penetration and ejaculation which accompanies the believer's copulation, contains the sperm of the Seed responsible for the begetting of the foetal Christ; and 3) the cessation of the *menstrual* flow is itself always a very important and pertinent piece of divine evidence in this vital connection. And thus, in summary, we have the expression of the threefold tell-tale "Witness of God" which every true believer subjectively experiences.

John is of course telling us that the begotten life automatically stops the blood-flow in the menstrual phenomenon. In our earthly bodies, we are aware that both phenomena—blood and conception—are linked together and synchronized. Without begettal, the menstrual flow keeps on; conversely, only a begettal (conception) can bring about its complete stoppage for the duration. The threefold "Witness of God" in the foregoing verses therefore comprehends the three essentials in the divine quickening—"the Spirit, the Water, and the Blood"—which thus bear infallible record of the fact that the Life of the Son in us gives us His Life, His Light, His Righteousness, and His Immortality, in full. All of which we further have in perpetuity, to hold and enjoy throughout the eons, starting here and now even in the present eon of "grace and truth,"—this being our eonian life!

"Therefore being buried with Him by baptism into His death" symbolically transfers the blood-guilt of His crucifixion by wicked, malevolent, and unregenerate hands from our own to other shoulders; and being of Him and in Him, and so identified with Him in the cruel scourging, crucifixion, and death which He suffered, we can bravely and unabashedly plead "Not guilty as charged!" Being in His glorious celestial Body exculpates us from all guilt, even as accessories before and after the fact. On the other hand, all without the Living Body of Christ will have to answer in the Judgment which comes hereafter for what He suffered on Calvary. And being identified with Him in His Resurrection, of course, further relieves us of all guilty participation in His bloody crucifixion and death, as it relaxes us of all tension, anxiety, and fear therefor. Only the Divine Begettal can clear us from our responsibility in that awful bloody transaction. Thus for us as *begotten believers* the blood-flow entirely ceases and there is no guilt chargeable against us on the divine Books of Life.

In the brand-new life we *now* have with Him through "the Power of His Resurrection," we have the threefold evidence within ourselves which is itself the crowning achievement and infallible Witness of the divine quickening. For verily it begets *"a lively Hope"* within us of the certainty and the reality of our New Birth at the instant of our mortal death! Let no believer dare to question the divine record on this matter and so make God out "a liar!" Let every believer who has the wellspring of the Life of the Son in him accept this as tangible proof that "the Witness of God" abides in him. Let us therefore *"believe the record that God gave of His Son"*:

> "These things have I written unto you that believe on THE NAME of the Son of God: that ye may know that ye *have* eonian life, and that ye may believe on THE NAME of the Son of God [namely, the precious Name LORD JESUS CHRIST]."—I John 5:13 and cf. Matthew 28:19 and Philippians 2:10, 11.

IV

The Messianic Kingdom Established and the Life Hereafter

30. *Commentary on John 3:1-12*

AT THIS POINT IN OUR THEMATIC DEVELOPMENT, WE COME TO the igneous or burning crux of *The New Birth* which at once is the sublime key to its correct appraisal and approach as well as being the key to the necessary spiritual insight into the meaning of the *Kingdom of God*. Moreover, it gives us the key which unlocks the mystery of the Messianic Kingdom as this relates to its establishment in the invisible realm of the heavens and to the divine operations in its three domains or spheres, together with its corollary dating in the apostolic era. As unfolded, it enables us to perceive the reality of some of the strange, weird phenomena in our surrounding universe, more or less metaphysical or psychical in nature and manifestation, which mystify and baffle us and otherwise remain inexplicable. It therefore enables us to perceive the existence as well as the reality of such things *in our very midst,* some of them admittedly spine-tingling, blood-curdling, and downright eerie and spooky. The key to the New Birth is the wondrous mystic key which both unlocks and unfolds all this, as we now give particular attention to John 3:1-12.

The correct rendering of these verses is its own correct interpretation and is important to an understanding of many aspects of the Kingdom of God including the New Birth itself, hitherto unsuspected or misunderstood, and especially as this relates to the Passion of the Risen Lord underscored in Acts 1:2, 3 "by many infallible proofs." As culled from *The Companion Bible*, which provides distinct illumination, same is now appended with notes and commentary following. The Bible student should bear in mind that every occurrence in this passage, in the A.V., of the word "born" is in the Greek *gennao*, and as previously shown should be consistently given the translation "begotten." We read:

"1) There was a man of the Pharisees, named Nicodemus, a ruler of the Jews: 2) the same came to Jesus by night, and said unto Him, Rabbi, we know that Thou art a Teacher come from God: for no man can do these miracles that Thou doest except God be with him. 3) Jesus answered and said unto him, Verily, verily, I say unto thee, Except a man be *begotten again,* he cannot see the Kingdom of God. 4) Nicodemus saith unto Him, How can a man be *begotten again* when he is old? can he enter the second time into his mother's womb, and be *begotten?* 5) Jesus answered, Verily, verily, I say unto thee, Except a man be *begotten* of THE SPIRIT'S WATER [literally, The Spirit's *seminal water;* hence being *Spiritual Water,* which is Living Water from THE SPIRIT'S own belly and in divine meaning the *sperm* or seed of the begettal], he cannot enter into the Kingdom of God. 6) That which *has been begotten* of the flesh [i.e., of fleshly water, or semen] is flesh; and that which *has been begotten* of THE SPIRIT [namely, of Spiritual Water, this again being the semen in the Living Word] is spirit. 7) Marvel not that I said unto thee, Ye must be *begotten again!* 8) THE SPIRIT [being as invisible as *wind,* but just as literal in its Essence] bloweth where it pleaseth, and thou hearest the sound thereof, but canst not tell whence it cometh, and whither it goeth: so is every one that is *begotten* of THE SPIRIT. 9) Nicodemus answered and said unto

Him, How can these things be? Jesus answered and said
unto him, Art thou a *teacher* of Israel, and knowest not
these things? 11) Verily, verily, I say unto thee, We speak
that we do know, and testify that we have seen; and ye receive not our witness. 12) If I have told you earthly things,
and ye believe not, how shall ye believe, if I tell you of
heavenly things?"

Of verse 4 *The Companion Bible* says: "Of course, Nicodemus misunderstands and uses the word *gennao* of the
mother; the Lord uses it of the Father, as meaning begetting." Hence the rebuke which he receives. He is, in effect,
consequently reproved as follows:

"Are you a Teacher—or Master—in Israel and yet incap-
able of perceiving the distinction between earthly and heavenly phenomena? If you are thus unable properly to dis-
tinguish the purely physical aspects of this question as it
relates to the reciprocal roles of father and mother—that one
is the active partner in generation, hence doing the begetting; whereas the other is simply the passive partner, and
hence doing the bringing forth—then how can you possibly
be expected to comprehend the higher, more vital, and indeed the mystical and elusive aspects of the subject when
dealing with it on a wholly intangible and quite invisible
basis?"

Thus rebuked, he is forthwith told by Jesus, "Verily we
speak according to what we do know, and hence according
to what we do see and can understand in the natural." However, that was still not enough and Nicodemus is left as un-
comprehending as ever, even as many like him today still
are. Of course, this was Spiritual Biology in a sense and with
a significance that Nicodemus didn't know anything about,
neither his contemporaries and successors of that period
nor his compeers of the present.

Of verse 5: "Begotten of Water and of the Spirit" (A.V.)

—the crux of the New Birth—is literally "of Water and Spirit," however with this differentiation: As there is no article in the Greek before Spirit, the phrasing in the original therefore comprehends, not the concept or idea of two distinct things (water and Spirit), *but in fact of just one,* hence giving us *Spiritual Water* instead. In this perspective of the Greek, the latter noun (Spirit) becomes an emphatic adjective, determining the meaning and nature of the former noun (water), and showing that the single thought divinely focussed—the exact one in the divine purview—is the "Spirit's Water!" The Greek is to be rendered *"of water—yea, Spiritual Water."* In this connection, John 7:38, 39 is the clue to the mystery of the Spirit's seminal inflow of gushing water (the ejaculation), as presented in the following divine illumination covering the Saviour's own words and the inspired comment upon same in the own words of the disciple recording same. We read:

> "38) He that believeth on Me, as the Scripture hath said, out of *HIS Belly* [whose? namely, THE SPIRIT'S BELLY, as interpreted in the next verse] shall flow rivers of living water [hence, *the Spirit's seminal Water,* this being Spiritual Water," the disciple John then adding in explanation of this divine euphemism], "39) *But this spake He of the Spirit* [namely, *Himself* being the *to Pneuma to Hagion*] which they that believe on Him should receive: for *The Holy Spirit* was not yet given, *because that Jesus was not yet glorified."* (Cf. John 14:26; 15:26; 16:13-19; Acts 1:4, 5; 2:1-4; Revelation 5:6, with which also cf. II Corinthians 3:17.)

Of verse 6: In the Greek, the tense here has changed its form to the Perfect from the simple Aorists in verses 3, 4, 5, 7, and therefore indicates the completion of the action in the begettal—hence signifying "birth," i.e., "born."

Of verse 8: "Wind" in the A.V. is properly "the Spirit." The word *pneuma* occurs 385 times, and is rendered "wind" only here, but elsewhere (384 times!) it is "spirit." Hence, it should be translated "the Spirit" as at end of verse. "Wind" is *anemos*, a quite different word. It occurs 31 times, and is always so rendered.

The allusion in the entire context of John 3:1-12 was, of course, to the resurrection from the dead, being expressed in the divine terminology of *birth* into the Kingdom of God. But Nicodemus did not comprehend its meaning; neither did the disciples; and neither do many Christians today. An intensive course of indoctrination and training—connoted under the designation of "His Passion"—had to be undertaken by the Master in order to bring His apostles into the light of this special meaning, as we shall presently see under our next topical consideration.

In the foregoing commentary, we have the key which definitively unlocks the meaning of Romans 8:29; Colossians 1:15, 18 and Revelation 1:5 (R.V.), with respect to the Resurrected Christ. Accordingly, as Acts 1:2, 3 tells us, being at this time "the Firstborn from the dead," He appeared at various times and places, under varying circumstances, "unto the apostles whom He had chosen," to whom "He showed Himself *alive* [or BORN from the dead!] *after His Passion* by many infallible proofs, being seen of them forty days *and speaking of the things pertaining to the Kingdom of God.*" This He did in the assiduous and devoted way divinely called "His Passion," in the burning and successful attempt and with the fiery zeal of earnestness and enthusiasm to drill into their slowly perceiving consciousness and minds what being initially begotten and then subsequently born into the Kingdom of God could only mean.

It is significant, moreover, that He used the occasion of the Feast of Pentecost, which they were even then celebrating in the memorable year of grace A.D. 31, to demonstrate the fact of His Resurrection and the reality of His aliveness after the event called death, which He did by many significant evidences, called "infallible proofs," during forty exciting days of this festivity. Thus He sought to inculcate in them an unquestionable awareness, which led slowly, after forty days, to the moment of final success and to their full comprehension, of the vital meaning of John 3:1-12 in relation to the entire subject of the *New Birth, of which it is verily the divine key.*

31. The "Infallible Proofs" as Further Related to "His Passion"

Apropos of Acts 1:2, 3, the "infallible proofs" which the risen Saviour was to present to His apostles consisted of a series of divine manifestations covering His remarkable appearances and His equally sudden and mysterious disappearances, all of which were nicely calculated to lead them gently, patiently, understandingly, cogently, surely, imperceptibly, unerringly, and at last triumphantly from the known to the unknown, from the natural to the spiritual, from the earthly to the heavenly, from the material to the ethereal, from the mysterious to the comprehensible, and thus from the historical JESUS and His earthbound, earth-limited range of operations, to Himself as the etherealized omnipresent CHRIST of glory, or seven-horned Lamb, who becomes "shed abroad" as the Indwelling Presence. As such, in turn, He becomes "Another Comforter," namely, the *Paraclete*, so that, with this ultimate transformation before them and being gradually conditioned thereto, His disciples in all subsequent time might both discern and comprehend the essential meaning and purpose and nature of the Kingdom mystery. As demonstrated, the "infallible proofs" were further designed to acquaint His immediate disciples little upon little, degree upon degree, with the positive realization that, even like the invisible wind, "the Spirit [namely, Himself] bloweth where it listeth, and thou hearest the sound thereof, but canst not tell whence it cometh, and whither it goeth: *so is every one that is begotten of the Spirit.*" (Romans 5:5; Ephesians 4:10; Revelation 5:6 and II Corinthians 3:17.)

In John 20:30 His various manifestations, transformations and demonstrations are stated to be "signs," hence evidences symbolic, figurative and illustrative of the kind of invisible activity—invisible to mortal apperception and vision, that is —that the Kingdom of God *per se* represents. More and more He manifests Himself to His disciples as the invisible Presence and less and less in His bodily apparatus, until by the end of forty days He at last approaches the peak of invisibility, being then ready to ascend into His celestial permanence and universality. Thus see-sawing back and forth, He ascends into Heaven where He is thereafter lost in *total invisibility,* being once again in the glory which He had with the Father before the Disruption.

The lesson that He is no longer to be thought of in terms of the historical Jesus—that is to say, after the flesh—becomes at last indelibly impressed and seared into their memory and minds and becomes firmly grounded and rooted into their consciousness. Only as the Universal Comforter after the Spirit—the *Paraclete*—is He now to be thought of and apprehended, in terms of His being *the Holy Spirit of promise!* "Yea," says the Apostle Paul, "though we have known Christ after the flesh, yet now henceforth know we Him so no more." (Cf. II Corinthians 5:16; I Timothy 1:17; 6:15, 16; Colossians 1:15; Hebrews 11:27 and John 17:5, 24.)

Accordingly, the further lesson becomes solidly embedded and deeply entrenched into their hearts and minds where it becomes enshrined, that being *exclusively Spirit*—that is to say, being at last the invisible Spirit in His glorified Essence—He is thus on our part no longer to be dealt with, or to be apprehended or understood, as a physical presence alone (that being now thankfully past) but wholly and even more importantly and vitally as a rarefied, etherealized, universal, invisible Celestial Presence in the form of THE LIVING CHRIST cosmically. The Cosmic Christ is identically expressed in the form of His local and personal Indwelling, whereby manifold miniature invisible Christs become *literally* begotten and formed into all true believers in Him and in "the Power of His Resurrection." It is thus that organically and biologically we have the proliferation of the true Vine and its branches, which in turn expresses the celestial BODY OF CHRIST, otherwise the *Kingdom of God!*

With a continuing demonstration of this transformation which occupied the forty days of His Passion, covering a pattern of Himself which is first in one form and then the other, alternatingly visible and invisible, the physical Jesus at last becomes ready for His ascension into the sphere of the heavenlies—hereafter the realm of His utter invisibility and celestial glory. It is in this celestial realm where His bodily apparatus and His fleshly antecedents and circumstances, with their earthly limitations in time and space, recede and vanish into the background, becoming altogether lost from the visible level of His humanity and becoming fully transformed into the invisible level of His universal Spirit Essence. And it is from this celestial vantage point, or perch, that He can then operate everywhere and at once, which is to say, cosmically, as the manifested Indwelling Presence, in order "to fill all things." Like the TV transmitter within the range of our mortal senses and of our everyday acquaintance and surroundings, He can thus image Himself upon our heart-screens and so beget the foetal or new creature—"Christ in you!" And also He can thus pluck and vibrate our heartstrings through the Divine Quickening, and in this divine way, we will be able to perceive that the very cockles of our hearts have been strangely warmed.

The witness of "His Passion," which is also the witness of the fulfillment of the coming Messianic Kingdom in their midst, the witness of its existence and arrival, and the witness of its reality and vitality, becomes fully demonstrated on Pentecost itself, the fiftieth day of its festal celebration. For it was on this occasion that "suddenly there came the sound from heaven as of a rushing mighty wind [or blast, Gr. *pnoe*], *and the Christ of God Himself in the form of the Holy Spirit* filled all the house where the disciples were sitting and they were filled [being exactly *sealed* as they were] with His actual and literal Indwelling Presence." (Acts 2:1-4 and cf. II Corinthians 1:22; Ephesians 1:13 and 4:30.)

All of the "infallible proofs of His Passion" (and there were of course many such, as told in John 20:30 and 21:25) were given to demonstrate His own aliveness after death, especially in view of the attribute and quality of evanescence which He brought into display by His manifestations and transformations as these became more and more pronounced, and even more and more dazzling. Starting from Pentecost A.D. 31 (and especially as pertaining to the establishing of the Kingdom of God which, as divinely reckoned, synchronizes with this very year), life after death—meaning the New Birth—becomes brought to light through the Gospel, as Paul reveals in II Timothy 1:10. And as we have hitherto seen, this is exactly the state of *derived or imputed Immortality* for all who believe in the Name of the Son, the matchless name LORD JESUS CHRIST, and none other. (I Timothy 1:9, 10; I Corinthians 6:9-11; Ephesians 5:5; Revelation 21:8 and 22:15.) Again, this is the state of uninterrupted continuity in the existence and life which *all believers in His Name* forthwith acquire when they become "begotten again." Hence, at the subsequent "birth" (which is the phenomenon we call death), they inherit bodies from heaven which thereafter enable them to come and go like the invisible wind, even as the Living Christ Himself could demonstrate the truth of this to His own apostles—their very eyes beholding and witnessing the fact of His aliveness from the dead "by many infallible proofs," though at first they were unbelieving.

In this connection, we read in Luke 24:36-41 of the occasion when He suddenly and quite mysteriously "stood in the midst of them," and of how "they were terrified and affrighted, and supposed that they had seen a spirit [or apparition]. And He said unto them, Why are ye troubled? and why do thoughts arise in your hearts? Behold my hands and my feet, *that it is I Myself!* Handle Me and see [find out for yourselves]; for a spirit [an apparition] hath not flesh and bones, as ye see Me have." The record, continuing, discloses that, while overjoyed, they still didn't want to believe. We come to the conclusion from the foregoing that it is on the plane of supernatural existence that believers everywhere are hence plainly assured: "thou hearest the sound thereof, but canst not tell whence it cometh and whither it goeth."

The pattern of His own Resurrection, in which His own flesh and bones, minus His blood, were included was, of course, the pattern for all Israel as connected to their Old Covenant relationship, and is the one focussed in Ezekiel 37, which exactly projects them in a state of resurrection, or birth, "in the midst of the valley which was full of [dry] bones"—namely, as with Him, flesh plus bones minus blood. But for the New Creation in Christ Jesus which was imminent with the close of the apostolic generation and so with the end of the Old Testament age (A.D. 70), a new order of things under the New Covenant relationship becomes envisaged and henceforth inaugurated, as unveiled by the Apostle Paul throughout all his epistles. Consequently, we find A.D. 70 dating a clearly celestial (as opposed to flesh and bones) creation *in Him* in which all the "old things are passed away and, behold, all things are become new,"—this being indeed the very heart and pith of the Faith-Gospel.— II Corinthians 5:17.

In keeping with this vital prospect, Paul was able to declare that flesh and blood (plus bones) could not enter into the inheritance of the Kingdom of God, but instead, we have brought to light the new spirit-nucleus or germ and the new celestial-type body which are the believer's through justification by faith, which derives everything from Him —all brand-new and all a free divine gift!—I Corinthians 15:50.

The Master Himself refers to this new celestial inheritance in terms of the "many mansions in His Father's house" where He told His disciples He would go to prepare a place for them and where, through the Gospel which they were henceforth to proclaim, He would be also preparing a place for many believers in His Name who would be "begotten again" through "the Power of His Resurrection," adding "if it were not so, I would have told you!" How much more forthright and candid, frank and honest and emphatic concerning the blessed certainty of celestial bodies in the Hereafter could the Divine Instructor be! And yet we find among certain Christian circles those who dispute Him on this point and who teach otherwise—in effect, making Him out "a liar," as though He did not know what He was talking about! Howbeit, *still stands the Word! "If it were not so, I would have told you!"* And to this Paul further testifies in corroboration, saying:

> "For we know that if our earthly house of this tabernacle were dissolved [referring to the Adamic carcass with its constituents of flesh and blood and bones with which the Adamic mortal soul is clothed], we have a building of God [namely, the same heavenly *mansion* previously underscored by Jesus Himself to be in His Father's celestial abode], an house not made with hands, eonian in the heavens. For in this [mortal frame or mansion] we groan, earnestly desiring to be clothed upon with our house [or mansion] which is from heaven: if so be that being clothed we shall not be found naked [as in the *gumnon-kokkon,* which Paul also writes about in I Corinthians 15:37, 38]. For we that are in this tabernacle do groan, being burdened: not for that we would be unclothed, *but clothed upon* [as I Corinthians 15: 38 tells us, and hence to be *made perfect* as Hebrews 12:23 also tells us], that mortality might be swallowed up of life." (John 14:1-4 and II Corinthians 5:1-4, with which cf. John 14:26.)

The indubitable evidence thus divinely accorded by the Master Demonstrator further underscores the aliveness of all believers passing into the celestial sphere of the Hereafter through the portal of the Begettal, which is in turn realized through justification by faith in "the Power of His Resurrection." The reality of it all becomes divinely assured, in spite of its utter invisibility to those still remaining upon the earthly scene in Adamic bodies, who "have not the Spirit of Christ." These having eyes and seeing not and so being purblind, and also being "dead in trespasses and sins," are hence unperceiving and exactly unaware of the meaning of "Life only in Christ Jesus!" (Cf. Romans 8:9-11 and I John 5:8-13.)

The "infallible proof" to believers today is accordingly perceived in the fact of the Begettal, followed with the divine quickening, whereby "together with Christ, God hath raised us up together, and made us sit together [as celestials] in heavenly places in Christ Jesus," meaning therefore in the Celestial BODY OF CHRIST synonymous with the invisible Kingdom of God, in which as of now and in this present eon, "God hath set the members every one of them in THE BODY, as it hath pleased Him!" (I Corinthians 15: 45; I Peter 1:3 and II Corinthians 12:18.)

The conclusion is therefore inescapable that the Passion of the Risen Lord, being the insatiable desire which He had "to give the light of the knowledge of the glory of God in the face of Jesus Christ" (II Corinthians 4:6), was the infallible demonstration needed to thoroughy convince and acquaint His immediate disciples, and all reluctant believers since, of the divine facts of life. Among them is this, that when "born" at death, one can be very much a live being with a celestial-type body who can come and go like the wind, and still be wholly invisible to mortal sight and apprehension, and otherwise to the mortal perception and awareness of all others upon the human scene of existence and activity. And the knowledge of this today comes only through the act of faith—*just simply believing*—in Him, and in His Name, and in "the Power of His Resurrection."

32. *The Unveiling of the Messianic Kingdom*

The Feast of Pentecost in A.D. 31 definitely marked the transition that was henceforth to take place from the natural to the spiritual state and from the earthly, temporal form of existence to the celestially permanent (or eonian) form, whereby believers everywhere would become con-

scious of their new estate in the life of the Son of God, as
that life is hidden and staked therein. The means of salvation as well as the avenue of entrance into the Kingdom
of God are hence more clearly focussed and more thor-
oughly understood as a result of the transcendent Passion of
the Risen Lord and the devotion and skill, intensity and
zeal, which He (being the Son of God with all the divine re-
sources, perquisites and prerogatives inherent to same)
could bring to its remarkable demonstration, and which
succeeded so well in opening the minds of His apostles to
the equally transcendent implications and ramifications of
the subject. It is through His Passion that believers in all
time since Pentecost should also gain the spiritual perception, together with the insight and depth, necessary to acquaint them with the divine facts of their life in Him. And
among the facts connected with this divine life would be
none more crucial and noteworthy, and indeed none more in-
triguing and spellbinding, than the contemplation that
"though we have known Christ after the flesh [when He
was Jesus of Nazareth, which includes His Palestinian background as well as all His earthly activities], *yet now henceforth know we Him so no more.*"—II Corinthians 5:16. The
contemplation of this divine fact of life should, for all believers, be a moment of grandeur—a glorious moment of up-
lifting and spiritual exaltation!

We are divinely told that His Passion was directed to
one over-riding holy purpose, the evidence of which is seen
in the fact that all His energies were concentrated in "speaking of the things pertaining to the Kingdom of God." It is
accordingly in this light that we can be sure that the apostles themselves, in turn, concentrated on proclaiming the
vital message of the Kingdom to the nations in terms of
the selfsame specialized meaning and approach, and with
the selfsame specialized emphasis, which He Himself
brought to its spiritual elucidation and to the practical aspects of its visual demonstration. And like Paul who, in the
same frame of reference as envisaged in both John 3:1-12

and Acts 1:2, 3, went about *"preaching the Kingdom of God,* and teaching those things which concern the Lord Jesus Christ, with all confidence, no ·man forbidding him," so to believers everywhere the due arrival and establishment of the Messianic Kingdom in the apostolic era, together with all the current aspects of its eonian functioning and phasing, should no longer be a matter of continuing mystery or of uncertainty, doubt, or speculation, but instead should be a matter of deep and special, and of intensive and abiding concern to each and every one.

As a sidelight to our approach, we have to keep before us the occasion when, led before Pilate by the chief priests who accused Him of falsely double-talking Himself as the King of the Jews, "Jesus answered, My Kingdom is not of this world [Gr. *kosmos*], then would My servants fight, that I should not be delivered to the Jews: *but now is My Kingdom not from hence!"*—John 18:33-36. That, too, should be plain to believers everywhere (excluding those who are not in the Spirit). The Messianic Kingdom in which the Son would reign has no direct relevancy (except where the need of special divine intervention or interposition in certain situations requires some degree of celestial over-ruling, to the honor and glory of God) with the present visible theater of human activities and operations—our world! Hence, to the Jews and others who sought to lay bloody hands upon Him and succeeded so well in their cruel attempts, it wasn't to be too long, either, before He would be meeting them again in that Kingdom which would be His, the very Kingdom they were scornfully pooh-poohing and the very King they were scornfully rejecting. In other words, He was referring to the state of invisible operations which would spell the Hereafter, this meaning the Judgment of souls which to every man and woman comes with the hour which tolls the knell of mortal doom. And Psalms 2:4, 5 gives us a further inkling of what would be happening to these unfortunate Jews at the renewal of their meeting with Him in His Kingdom. For it is on this solemn level, whether they wanted

to believe it or not, when "He that sitteth in the heavens
shall laugh: the Lord shall have them in derision. Then shall
He speak unto them in His wrath, and vex them in His sore
displeasure." (Revelation 19:15, 16; 11:15-17; I Corinthians
15:24, 25; Philippians 2:9-11, with which cf. Daniel 2:35, 44;
Hebrews 9:27 and Proverbs 1:24-33.)

In the light of John 3:1-12 and Acts 1:2, 3, the Book of
the Revelation is now seen as the indubitable unveiling of
the Messianic Kingdom of the Lord Jesus Christ, which only
those, like John, *in the Spirit* and having the Mind of Christ
dwelling in them can enter, if they would grasp its deep significance and its underlying message. It is this Book which,
being the perfect divine key, alone unlocks the secrets pertaining to the mystery of the Hereafter. The Book itself
spreads before us a panorama of celestial activity which
only those having the key can grasp in the fullness of its
invisible operations. It spreads before the believer the certainty and reality of the Hereafter which at once follows
mortal death—a Hereafter teeming, humming, and peopled
with existence and with the activities of live sentient beings
come to Judgment and otherwise functioning in keeping
with the type of celestial rewards divinely meted out.

The Book of the Revelation therefore spreads before us
the divine panorama of the Kingdom of the Heavens in its
threefold dimensions—a Kingdom that is eonian in duration,
in which the Son is now, and has been ever since A.D. 70,
reigning as King of Kings and Lord of Lords. It is there he
subdues all enemies of the Cross and all hostile forces of the
Gospel, ruling them with a rod of iron and eventually grind-
ing them into willing submission and obedience to Him,
until the grand climax in the eons is reached which is the
consummation of all things. And it is at this critical eonian
juncture that, we are divinely assured, "at the Name of
Jesus [even at the merest whisper or mention of it and the
least flicker of its sounding] every knee should bow, of
things in heaven, and of things in earth, and of things under
the earth: and that every tongue should confess that Jesus

Christ is Lord to the glory of God the Father."—Philippians 2:10, 11.

Hence, it is at this point, when the Grand Finale is ushered in, that the Son, who hitherto was given the authority to be Head over all things, Himself becomes subject, even to God the Father. And it is *then*, we next read: ". . . when He shall have delivered up the Kingdom to God, even the Father: when He shall have put down all rule and all authority and power. . . . And when all things shall be subdued unto him, *then* [!] shall the Son also be subject unto Him that put all things under Him, *that God may be All-in-All!*"—I Corinthians 15:24-28.

Without going into a detailed breakdown and analysis (impossible within the allotted scope of our discussion) of the Book of the Revelation, which in over-all perspective is the unveiling of the invisible activity going on in the Hereafter, suffice it if we call attention to the fact that, again in the light of John 3:1-12 and Acts 1:2, 3, Jesus the Son of God is now reigning and ruling in the Kingdom which was initially set up in connection with the first ascension at the opening of Pentecost, A.D. 31. And from A.D. 70 when the last of the Seven Trumpets sounded, He thereafter received all rights and full authority from the Father as King of Kings and Lord of Lords. For it was when "the seventh angel sounded that there were heard great voices in heaven, saying, The Kingdom [i.e., Sovereignty] of this world [the inhabited world of human dwelling, experience, and activity] is become the Kingdom of our Lord [God the Father] and of His Christ [the Son of God]: and He [the Son] shall reign [or rule] to the eons of the eons."—Revelation 11:15.

And this is where we must leave Him *now*, in His Messianic Kingdom, the King in His Glory who is the Absolute Monarch and Sovereign Majesty over His whole universal dominion. Wherefore, in the words of the great apostle to the nations, we can also say with him: "Now unto the King eonian [the King of the ages, that is], immortal, invisible, the only wise God, be honor and glory to the eons of the

eons." (I Timothy 1:17, and cf. 6:14-16 and Revelation 19:
16.)

33. *The Kingdom of the Heavens*

By way of a brief restatement of the preceding findings
in the light of John 3:1-12 and Acts 1:2, 3, the now crucified
and Risen Saviour, beginning with Easter Sunday, utilizes
the Feast of Pentecost in order to dramatize the *beginning*
of His Messianic Kingdom. This He wonderfully accom-
plishes in the workings of His transcendent Passion, through
which He succeeds in *"shewing Himself ALIVE by many
infallible proofs unto the apostles whom He had chosen,
being seen of them forty days, and speaking of the things
pertaining to THE KINGDOM OF GOD."* The true "Lent-
en" season (of rejoicing rather than of sorrowing) therefore
comes after and not before Easter, representing as it does
the most solemn and momentous occasion in all Christian
history. For it was during this Pentecostal period of fifty
days that the Risen Son of man unfolded Himself in the
true dedication of His Passion, through which He seeks
to bring about an unquestioning understanding and perfect realization of the meaning of the Kingdom of God.
This He demonstrates in sober outlook and telescopic
sweep as He ranges down the eons of continuing time—
with deep longing and heartfelt tenderness, with insatiable
hunger and thirst, with passionate yearning and consuming
desire, with steadfast devotion and unflagging energy, with
utmost zeal and unceasing endeavors. And, best of all, this
too was applicable not only to the apostles immediately
present with Him but to all other believers everywhere and
since, in whom He thus seeks to trigger an invincible faith
and *"a lively hope"* in the meaning and attainment of the
Kingdom as members together in the same celestial Body.

As recorded in the ensemble by the four Gospel his-
torians of His earthly life and activities, His glorious Passion
involved certain mysterious appearances and disappearances,
one after the other in swift and dazzling succession, which

were all necessary adjuncts of the same divine transaction
in order to underscore the fact of the mystery of how He
could be the Ubiquitous and Omnipresent Christ. Alternat-
ing between materializing Himself on the one hand and
then swiftly etherealizing His Presence on the other hand,
these vanishing acts on His part were thus contrived to convey to the onlooker the quizzical impression "Now you see
Him!" and "Now you don't see Him!" while yet He was
around in person every moment of the time. All of this was
intended to spell out to His apostles the meaning, purpose,
and nature of the Kingdom of God, which was to all practical intents *already present* in their very midst. They as
Firstfruits of the Resurrection Harvest even then imminent
in its fullness, would in fact be its first celestial charter
members, being, as such, "Christ the Firstfruits!" (Cf.
Romans 8:22, 23 and James 1:18, and cf. I Corinthians 15:
23.) All of which, moreover, divinely wraps up "His Passion"
in its most glorious dynamic expression. In this aspect of its
great unfolding mystery, the establishment and unveiling of
the Messianic Kingdom becomes pegged to the whole Feast
of Pentecost itself. And the initial functioning of the Celestial Body of Christ, organicaly speaking, becomes dated from
the Great Tribulation in A.D. 70, Zion's travailing, and thus
brings into correct perspective the fullness of the glory of
Pentecost.

The Body of Christ is a distinctive creation, divinely
originated and fashioned, which in its totality represents
"a people for His Name" to be taken out of the uncircumcised nations or Gentiles. (Acts 15:14 and Romans 1:1-6.)
Its distinguishing characteristic lies in the fact that it is a
wholly *celestial* creation, and, as such, must be carefully distinguished from the circumcised people representing the
fleshly descendants of Abraham who are otherwise destined
for earthly habitation, hence being a *terrestrial* creation.

"And to this agree the words of the prophets, as it is
written: After this I will return, and will build again the

Tabernacle of David which is fallen down [now, alas, in ruins at the site of Jerusalem since A.D. 70, but happily *in God's set time* rebuilt]; and I will build again the ruins thereof, and I will set it up: that the residue of men might seek after the LORD, [including even] ALL THE GENTILES upon whom My Name is called, saith the LORD who doeth all these things."—Acts 15:15-17.

"God hath not cast away His people which He foreknew . . . For I would not, brethren, that ye should be ignorant of this mystery, lest ye should be wise in your own conceits: that blindness in part is happened to Israel, *until the fullness of the nations be come in* [namely, the Gentiles]. And so ALL ISRAEL [Abraham's fleshly descendants, that is] shall be saved: as it is written, *There shall come out of Zion* [being Celestial Jerusalem] THE DELIVERER, who shall turn away ungodliness from Jacob: for this is My Covenant to them, when I shall take away their sins."—See Romans 11.

"Behold, your house [Temple at Jerusalem A.D. 70] is left unto you desolate. For I say unto you, Ye shall not see Me henceforth, till ye shall say, *Blessed is He that cometh in THE NAME OF THE LORD!*"—Matthew 23:38, 39.

In this connection, note also Ezekiel, chapters 40-44, and chapter 21 of Revelation. Only an understanding of the eons and their purpose can reconcile the above, which becomes firmed up in the Millennial Temple presented here.

Corresponding with the two great components of the Gospel initially unfolded to Abraham at Mount Moriah, to whom it was ratified with the Divine Oath of the Covenant *"in which it was impossible for God to lie,"* are thus these two distinctive and contrasting creations, one celestial, typed as the "stars" and the other terrestrial, typed as "the sands upon the seashore." These are both to head up, over the indeterminate stretch covering the eons of the eons, into one that is the Body of Christ and the other that we find described in Revelation 21:9 as "the Bride, the Lamb's Wife." The celestial creation, all brand-new in its constituents and composition, belongs to the Kingdom of God, located in the First Heaven where God sits; the terrestrial creation being allocated somewhere along in the course of the eons to the Second and Third Heavens, included in the Son's dominion. (Cf. Genesis 22:16-18; Galatians 3:8, 9; Matthew 10:1-7, and Luke 10:1-9.)

The three heavenlies or invisible regions over which the Son of man is currently exercising jurisdiction over the nations in the Judgment, reigning and ruling over them and further subduing them "with a rod of iron," thus comprehend "the Kingdom of the Heavens" where their divine judgment is *now* proceeding apace. And, as noted previously, the Son's rule in the Hereafter is also in conjunction with His "out-resurrected" Firstfruits who divinely function with Him as celestial administrators and as His deputies, and who therefore "follow the Lamb whithersoever He goeth." The Greek word *ouranos* for "heaven" (which in the singular is the translation given in A.V.) is in the plural, hence it is in this threefold zone of operations or sphere of invisible activity, under the selfsame divine rule, that *salvation through judgments,* namely, universal reconciliation, becomes ultimately achieved for all humanity. And so, when the consummation of all things is reached in the onward progression of the eons, "every knee shall bow and every tongue confess that JESUS CHRIST is LORD to the glory of God the Father." It is at this time that Revelation 21:24-27 becomes fulfilled!

Being faced with this frightfully dismaying eventuality in all its eonian implications, people would do well to consider that in duration *the Hereafter is longer than the Here and Now,* and that they will of course live considerably longer in the former than it is possible for them ever to live in the latter. If they would only realize that they cannot escape the inevitable future, no matter what they might want to do with their lives in the present state of existence, they would begin to change their living habits in accordance with the precept and mandates of the Golden Rule. They would then live in fear and constant trembling for what would lie ahead, in light of the meaning and purpose of the divine judgments through which the wicked and disobedient and unsaved will be taught the way of righteousness. "For when the Lord's judgments are in the earth, the inhabitants of the world will learn righteousness." (Isaiah 26:9, and cf. Revelation 19:15 and 2:27.) They would therefore take out the necessary insurance against the day of reckoning and wrath that would enable them to escape the crucible of Hellfire and Purgatory, even though same will prove beneficent and benign in its ultimate results. And they would thus accept, *in the Here and Now rather than in the Hereafter,* the salvation provided freely through the Cross and spilt blood of Jesus Christ the Lord and consequently afforded through the redemptive power of His Resurrection.

The emphasis of the present Bible study covering "The New Birth" is directed, however, to the First Heaven and the celestial creation allocated to it, *which includes us* and which is directed to the necessary conditions for our acceptance as believers into the Kingdom of God, or Body of Christ, as celestial inheritors and partakers thereof. Only those who are *begotten again,* and hence made all new all over again, can inherit or ever expect to enter this invisible Kingdom. Only these can therefore see and enter into this celestial Paradise, to enjoy its matchless perfection, its imperishable beauty, together with the immortality found only in "the Tree of Life which is in the midst thereof"—that Paradise which is the abode of God Himself! (Revelation 2: 7 and 22:2.) By divine constitution and definition, *the believer when "born"* is at last a distinguished member in the celestial domain of the invisible Kingdom of God, which is also the Body of Christ. Addressing us as "brethren" in verse 1, Paul adds the enchanting prospect embracing the glories of the Hereafter found in I Corinthians 2:9: "But as it is written, Eye hath not seen, nor ear heard, neither have entered into the heart of man, the things which God hath prepared for those who love Him." Could any believer in Him, and sharing in the abundant Life that is only in the Son, ask for more? Let us therefore revel in its contemplation! (See also Paul's almost rhapsodic explanation of the *"unsearchable riches of Christ"* connected with this unfathomable mystery which he gives in Ephesians 3:1-12.)

34. The New Birth—Résumé

As presented in John 3:1-12 and the several associated passages we have scanned in this study, *gennao* literally means the genesis (or earliest beginnings) of begettal, followed as this is by gestation or pregnancy, which is a waiting period in which growth manifests itself in numerous ways, all of them being unmistakable and certainly understandable. Hence we have *genesis in utero,* which is to say, growth within the womb, being of course invisible all the way through. The entity thus formed (begotten, conceived, or imaged), though otherwise externally manifested as it begins to grow and as it continues to develop and expand, is always invisible during this entire period of incubation covering its internal residency, this being true as a natural fact and true as a spiritual fact, hence being true both in the earthly and in the divine sense.

Moreover, there is invariably an internal witness of the event, manifested in the *quickening,* through which the begotten entity—the unseen foetus—announces the fact of existence and being, announces that it is alive and that it is present, that it is kicking and growing, as if to say *"Here am I!"* The inner signals quite infallibly corroborate the existence and presence of an entirely new identity within, this being the new creation (or new creature) which, at the moment and for the duration, lies completely unseen and hidden, hence being initially known only to the person experiencing the wonder and vitality of it.

In this pregnant condition, the believer is therefore "begotten!" And let there be no mistake or doubt, he has "the

Witness of God" within him which enables him to proclaim its message far and wide—*the fact of his divine quickening!* When used of the father, *gennao* means "to beget or engender." When used of the mother, *gennao* also means "born," hence "to produce and bring forth," in the manner of offspring. Only at the birth is the child liberated, for it is *then* the mother is delivered.—Luke 2:6, 7. In terms of Spiritual Biology, this period of incubation or gestation (covering conception, development and embryonic growth of the unseen and as yet unborn foetus, "Christ in you!"), exactly expresses the pre-natal state of the believer in grace, which in all cases precedes his birth as a celestial man. Also by a divine figure of speech, which anticipates the event as an accomplished fact and consequently ahead of its literal happening, the believer acquires at once the status in grace of an adopted son, and to correlate this he is privileged to consider himself "born." To the extent that he keeps himself dead in the flesh (having thereby mortified the affections, lusts, and deeds of the old Adamic man representing what he was *formerly*), the believer automatically acquires the status of adopted son and along with this he is at once divinely recognized as one thus "born from the dead"—which is of course all by anticipation! *But he therefore must watch out and govern himself accordingly!* He must act and perform as though he were already a celestial in the glory and as though he were face to face with the Majesty on high, being surrounded by the Lamb, the holy angels, and all the other immortals, and with this consciousness of his divine destiny, he must have his conversation and his affections at all times pitched in heaven. In short, he must live as a Christian should and not frustrate the Grace of God in him by which he has been begotten—*or else woe be unto him!* (Romans 4:17 and Galatians 2:20,21.)

As previously focussed at the outset of the present study, the words *prototokos* and *titko* signify the completion of birth, which is expressed in the phenomenon called parturition. Hence "being born," in the divine sense, simply instances the time of delivery when we leave this mortal frame of dust—the time which we call our mortal death—to become separated from all earthly constituents and entanglements of flesh and blood and bones, including the essential Adamic ingredient of the soul. The Apostle Paul expresses this meaning of childbirth in terms of the pains of labor, wherein as he puts it: "even we ourselves groan within ourselves, waiting for the adoption, to wit, the redemption of our body."—Romans 8:23. Accordingly, it is then when we do inherit and acquire our celestial-type bodies which descend from heaven, the gift of the Father through *the Power of the Resurrection* of His only Begotten Son, who was and is "the Firstborn from the dead."

The separation of the New Creation from and out of the old takes place at the instant hour of mortal death, bringing with it the lasting cleavage of the New (or Second) Adamic Creature in Christ Jesus from the womb (or matrix) of the dust of the old Adamic structure and nature.[1] And this is hence the divine phenomenon which is analogous to the phenomenon of parturition in earthly childbirth, and which therefore becomes to every believer in Christ Jesus the Lord his golden passport and verily his "New Birth" into the Kingdom of God. And by every divine right of heritage, he is at last a fellow-member in the Celestial Body of Christ. He is, in short, a full-fledged sibling (son or daughter, as the case may be) of "the General Assembly and Church of the First-

---

[1] This cleavage may also be expressed in terms of the severance of the umbilical cord, the temporal life-line and the only direct connecting link between the two. In Ecclesiastes 12:5-7, the same biological concept is further emphasized physiologically in terms of the mortal dissolution of spinal column, skull, heart, and entire motive power of soul or mind in the human anatomy; and occurring as such "because man goeth to his long home, and the mourners go about the streets: or ever the *silver cord* be loosed, or the *golden bowl* be broken, or the *pitcher* be broken at the fountain, or the *wheel* broken at the cistern. Then shall the dust return to the earth as it was: and the spirit [namely, *the new soul as MADE PERFECT*, the *gumnon-kokkon*] shall return unto God who gave it."

born," the "Firstborn" refering to—as Romans 8:29; Colossians 1:15, 18 and Revelation 1:5 (R.V.) tell us—Him who is the Son, the blessed Lord and Saviour Jesus Christ *Himself!* And having the *new soul* begotten into him, this being "the new man which after God is created in righteousness and true holiness," which is divinely stated to be "the spirit of a just man," he is therefore *a man justified by his faith.* And, accordingly, he finds himself with the complement of a redemption body from heaven whereby he is *"made perfect"* for celestial habitation. (Ephesians 4:24 and Hebrews 12:23.)

It is of course then, with "the manifestation of the sons of God," that we have the fullest expression and ultimate fulfillment of *"Life Only in Christ Jesus!"*—the focus of the seminal seed contained in the Gospel of salvation as we find this divinely enunciated in I John 5:11, 12, through which the New Creation is begotten. For all *true* believers, it is the gateway to the breathless excitements and the unending surprises and unalloyed grandeur which they find immediately confronting them and which, in perpetuity, they will hereafter be revelling in and enjoying. It is the blissful hour of rapture as it is also the supreme moment of blessed realization and ecstatic fruition, being indeed the time and occasion of literal New Birth into the fullness of eonian life and into the fullness of the inheritance of celestial and immortal glory. This accordingly brings us to the consummation of the theme in our present Bible study, embracing as it does the field of Spiritual Biology.

We are now ready to conclude our discussion with the following illuminating commentary drawn from *Studies in Revelation*, by Pastor Albert Smith of England, writing under the pen-name "Christodoulos-Beta." We quote from his chapter covering "The Manchild" (p. 103), as follows:

"Jehovah says to backsliding Israel, 'Return, O backsliding children, for I am a Husband to you;' and as this is spoken to the corporate Woman, the Manchild in a corporate capacity must represent the children of the great Spirit Father. Hence, the Manchild would be born again of the Spirit before they could enter the Kingdom of God. See Jeremiah 3:14 and John 3:5. The New Birth refers to the resurrection from the womb of the earth—*Hades,* or *Sheol.* Those born of the Spirit would be able to come and go like the wind, others not knowing whence they come or whither they go. See John 3:8. Nicodemus, as being the 'Teacher in Israel', ought to have understood this allusion to the resurrection; but he did not. Hence the reproof he received from the Master. Many wrongly consider conversion as the New Birth; but Peter shows it is rather the *Begettal* into the hope of the resurrection, after the pattern of Jesus' resurrection from the dead.'—I Peter 1:23."

"*Light obeyed bringeth light;*
Light resisted bringeth night.
Who will give us power to choose,
If the love of light we lose."

"*Blest, too, is he who can divine*
Where truth indeed does lie;
And dare to take the side that seems
Wrong to man's blindfold eye."

"4. And my speech and my preaching was not with the words of man's wisdom, but in demonstration of THE Spirit and of Power.

"5. That your faith should not stand in the wisdom of men, but in *the Power of God!*

"6. Howbeit we speak wisdom among them that are perfect: yet not the wisdom of this world, nor of the princes of this world, that come to nought:

"7. But we speak the wisdom of God in a mystery, *even the hidden wisdom,* which God ordained before the world unto our glory:

"8. Which none of the princes of this world knew: for had they known it, they would not have crucified the LORD of Glory.

"9. *But as it is written, Eye hath not seen, nor ear heard, neither have entered into the heart of man, the things which God hath prepared for them that love Him.*

"10. But God hath revealed them unto us by His Spirit: for the Spirit searcheth all things, yea, the deep things of God.

"11. For what man knoweth the things of a man, save the spirit of man which is in him? *even so the things of God knoweth no man, but the Spirit of God.*

"12. Now we have received, not the spirit of the world, but the Spirit which is of God: *that we might know the things that are freely given to us of God.*

"13. *Which things also we speak, not in the words which man's wisdom teacheth, but which THE HOLY SPIRIT teacheth,* comparing spiritual things with spiritual.

"14. But the natural man receiveth not the things of the Spirit of God: for they are foolishness unto him; neither can he know them, because they are spiritually discerned.

"15. But he that is spiritual judgeth all things, yet he himself is judged of no man.

"16. *For who hath known the Mind of the LORD, that he may instruct HIM?** *But we have THE MIND OF CHRIST!*"

---

* In other words, we don't instruct Him—*He instructs us!* See also I John 2:26, 27.

V

Appendices

APPENDIX I

BIOGRAPHICAL SKETCH

Born in 1889 in Trinidad, B.W.I., I have always had an unquenchable yearning for the higher—in fact, what might be called the celestial—things of life, especially as concerning the cultural aspects and most importantly the spiritual values. This had been instilled into the very warp and woof of my being by God-fearing parents. I was sent abroad at the age of fifteen to attend college (Union College, College View, Nebraska) in preparation for a medical missionary career. However, as a result of World War I overseas service and a growing, up-and-coming family, this training was halted in 1917 while I was attending Meharry Medical College (then in Walden University) in Nashville, Tennessee.

Since then I have used my talents variously, concentrating among many ups and downs in the field of teaching, writing and editing, and, of course, religious work. In the main, this covers an over all lifetime career as schoolteacher, pastor, evangelist, and government employe. I was in continuous employment in the federal service from 1927 until retirement in 1951 due to disability, but despite physical handicaps and other hardships, I have since managed to keep fairly busy in the work of promoting Christian fellowship. This is a purely non-denominational activity, privately supported, and, as may be gathered, is conducted in keeping with the message and principles of *The New Birth*.

And finally, the answer to the all-pervasive and inevitable query, as oft spoken as it is sometimes left unspoken, is herewith beautifully summed up in the following quote attributed to the *Metalogicus* of John of Salisbury (c. 1159 A.D.), which reads: *"We are midgets, standing on the shoulders of giants, and that's why we can see farther than they."* The thought implicit, I hope, takes care of those who still want to know in all seriousness and earnestness, *as though it really mattered,* "Are you by any chance a Greek and Hebrew scholar?" The answer is emphatically and unashamedly *"No!"*

Apropos of this elevated perch (even if the role undeniably smacks of parasitism), the author has in mind *The Companion Bible* of the Oxford University Press, whose panel of topnotch and dedicated Hebrew and Greek experts, including the most respected and scholarly Rev. E. W. Bullinger, D.D., on many fronts has proved a mighty tower of support and comfort in this extremely trying and crucial hour of need. They have contributed of their lore and scholarship in guiding me over many gaping and other wise looming pitfalls.

Biblically, the same idea of the divine boost accorded to spiritual midgets is found expressed in Matthew 11:25, 26, as follows:

> "At that time Jesus answered and said, 'I thank Thee, O Father, Lord of heaven and earth, because Thou hast hid these things from the wise and prudent, and hast revealed them unto babes. *Even so, Father: for so it seemed good in Thy sight!*'"

—C. A. C.

APPENDIX II

SUMMARY DIGEST

The gist of the discussion herein is that the Christian believer has, first of all, to be "begotten again" before he can even be "born again," this being in explicit terms what Nicodemus was told by the Great Teacher sent from God —the compelling urgency of which applies to us today no less than it did to him then. And as it was exactly underscored in this connection, the Divine Begettal is hence the *sine qua non* (or indispensable requirement) for seeing or entering into the Kingdom of God, this being the New Birth, which refers to the believer's resurrection from and out of the dead.

The word used in the conversation with Nicodemus was "begotten," not "born," and is the only word that makes sense when it is grasped that begettal must always come before birth. This can apply only to a *literal New Creation* in and through Christ Jesus, seeing of course that no man can enter his mother's womb a second time in order either to be begotten or born again.

As complete divine salvation is predicated only through the death of Christ and hence provided only through the accompanying fact of *His Resurrection Power,* the New Creation therefore comprehends a new order of things, *all* the old things being swept out of the way. This means *all* that is in the old Adamic man, with *all* his physical parts and soulish aspects, *all* his nature, impulses, and tendencies, and *all* his fleshly lusts and affections, together with *all* his sinful disabilities, propensities, and inheritances. The believer has to be *completely regenerated,* which means he has to be completely refurbished, from head to toe and from stem to stern. Every bit of the old, inherent Adamic creature, as represented by blood and flesh as well as bones,—in fact, every particle and every ingredient of the old body is thus replaced.—II Corinthians 5:17.

The divine regeneration accordingly provides him with something that he never had before, and could never have obtained, or captured, or generated on his own. It consequently provides him with an entire new self, an entire new identity, an entire new personality, an entire new soul, an entire new being, and an entire new everything, *including even an entire new body* which has to descend from heaven to overclothe his naked spirit at his mortal death, and includes also an entire new name which is to be his in glory. All of this, in terms of its divine origin, is "hid in Christ" for the believer and becomes his *Other Self!*

It is accordingly from this constructive divine approach and in this potential divine sense, considering "the Power of God," why Paul in Galatians 2:20 could say: "I am crucified with Christ: *nevertheless I live, yet not I, but Christ liveth in me;* and the life which I now live in the flesh I live by the faith of the Son of God, who loved me and gave Himself for me." The Apostle moreover discreetly hastens to mention, as he next does in verse 21, but *"I do not frustrate the Grace of God!"*

In brief, being begotten again refers to the gestation or incubation period which is the pre-natal state of the believer in grace covering his conversion, and which also gives him the status of *adopted son* through the Power of Him, "even God, who quickeneth the dead, and calleth those things which be not as though they were."—Romans 4:17. And *the New Birth* itself refers to the parturition and post-natal state of the believer covering his "resurrection from the dead" when sonship, in the reckoning of time, becomes manifested for him. This, as we have tried to underline, occurs at the very instant of mortal dissolution when the summons comes to inherit immortality and ascend to celestial glory, there to join the innumerable redeemed throng around the throne of God.

APPENDIX III

INCEPTION AND BACKGROUND

The conditions surrounding the inception of the present Bible study—*The New Birth*—are herewith set forth to answer the many inquiries received for additional enlightenment regarding its theme and background.

Quite some years ago, as the result of an intensive study of the types in the Levitical service of the Feast of Pentecost, the subject matter of the New Birth gradually evolved itself, highlighted by the progressive discovery that there were two distinct ascensions of our Lord brought to light in the inspired New Testament record. The *first ascension* is seen to be associated with the resurrection presented in Matthew 27:50-53, marking the occasion of the first day of this Pentecostal Feast as it was to occur in A.D. 31, in conjunction with the Crucifixion and the Feast of Passover which typed it. This specially resurrected group—whoever they were *and mindful of the fact that they are in heaven above NOW*—accordingly represented the Wave Sheaf offering allocated in the types to this day and, as such, divinely denominated the initial Firstfruits of the Old Testament Resurrection Harvest, typed by the Feast of Trumpets in turn. (Cf. Leviticus 23:9-22 and Deuteronomy 16:9, 10.)

With this preliminary discovery, I soon became aware that Firstfruits *per se* in any language inevitably pointed to an immediate chronological sequence, expressed in terms of a follow-up crop or succeeding general harvest, which as an invariable principle and rule always spell out the certainty of *more of the same* both in nature and in identity, not to mention texture and quality. The Feast of Trumpets was next seen to cover this latter expectation or prospect—the final phasing of the harvest cycle—thus leading to the conclusion that the Resurrection Harvest as pertaining to Old Testament Israel was divinely comprehended and exactly forecast in the two Levitical feasts covering Pentecost and Trumpets, and that both of these belonged exclusively to the same chronological period. Moreover, the relationship between Firstfruits and harvest compelled it to be so!

Accordingly, if one began to be fulfilled in A.D. 31 (which was true of the Feast of Pentecost), the latter was inevitably bound to be not very far behind in point of time (which was true of the Feast of Trumpets in A.D. 70). The inter-relationship between the picking of any Firstfruits and the ensuing harvest which it dates is one that is always exact, being direct and close, steadfast and constant, and hence inerrant and immutable, considered either in the earthly or in the divine sense, or from the standpoint of Natural or Spiritual Biology. Having put in its appearance, the initial set of Firstfruits unfailingly dates everything else connected with it, even the very crop itself. The chronological sequence of fruitage, as further exhibited in complementary Firstfruits, is therefore contemporary beyond all cavilling. Hence, as applied to the entire general Harvest Resurrection of Old Testament Israel denoted under the Feast of Trumpets, the initial Wave Sheaf of Matthew 27: 50-53 dated all the succeeding stages and sequences of its complete cycle, pinpointing same to the apostolic period between A.D. 31 and 70.

Inasmuch as in the Levitical types there were two complementary sets of Firstfruits projected for the Feast of Pentecost, one set belonging to the first day thereof and the other set to the fiftieth day, it at once became apparent that *the Day of Pentecost itself* represented the fulfillment of the expectation of the latter set of Firstfruits, as these were to be spotlighted in significant relationship to the *Second Ascension* with the downpour of "the Holy Spirit of promise" which of course fell on this fiftieth day, A.D. 31. There finally dawned the realization and the revelation concerning who these were, namely, the 144,000 *Hebrew Christians* repre-

senting the twelve tribes of ethnic or literal Israel and otherwise constituting the two Houses of *Israel* and *Judah* (as
such, the Two Wave Loaves), who were contemporaries of
Jesus and who became chosen, *sealed,* and then "out-resurrected" (the *exanastasis* of Philippians 3:11) as Firstfruits
in the Apostlic Generation. Moreover, as they are identified
as the fleshly descendants of Abraham, Isaac, and Jacob, who
were Christians by the confessions of the Name of Christ
(as pointed out in Revelation 12:17; 14:12 and 20:4 and
the several related passages of this *Book of the Unveiling of
Christ Jesus the Lord*), it proves that these Hebrews were
all Christians!

In the antitypes we find the initial group of Firstfruits,
in relation to the First Ascension, ascending as "captives" of
the Risen Son, who Himself, we are told, *"led captivity captive"*—an expression peculiarly relevant to the group resurrected in Matthew 27:50-53, who up to that point over the
long haul of the centuries had been held in the Stygian
gloom of darkness representing the captivity of Death and
the bondage of the Grave (Gr. *Thanatos* and *Hades*) as referred to in Revelation 1:18. (Cf. Ephesians 4:8 and note
marginal reading in the A.V.) The Wave offering in the
typical service was so-called because it was waved to and fro
by the priest, to become wafted aloft from the burning cen-
ser in his hand as ascending incense, or smoke, which finally
reaches heaven and the presence of God, the priest himself
prefiguring Christ and the incense in turn prefiguring those
ascending to be a sweet-smelling savour to the Father in
heaven.

Hence, as an offering (which was pegged to the first day
of the Feast of Pentecost, in contrast to the two Wave
Loaves pegged to the fiftieth day and representing the
Houses of Israel and Judah), the Wave Sheaf signified that
the initial sheaf of Resurrection Firstfruits, who thus ascended into heaven, was ushered into the Father's presence
to be accepted by Him, and that, with reference to the year
A.D. 31, this antitypical event took place on the first day of

the week, or Sunday, which was also (as it divinely had to be) the first day of this feast.

Further, in the Book of the Unveiling (see Revelation 4 and 5), the same resurrected group spotlighted in Matthew 27:50-53 becomes identified beyond any shadow of doubt as the four Beasts and the twenty-four Elders (otherwise the four Zoa and the twenty-four Presbyters). In other words, they were the Firstfruits of the Old Testament Resurrection Harvest, which itself, in point of chronology and sequence, could not be so very far behind its own initial Firstfruits. We have said before that this event had been forecast in sacred prophecy to occur at the time of Jacob's trouble (synonymous with Zion's travailing) as this was to occur in A.D. 70 with the Destruction of Jerusalem. (Cf. Daniel 9:24-27; 12:1-3; Ezekiel 37 and cp. Jeremiah 30:7 and Matthew 24:15-22.)

It was inevitable that I should reach the conclusion, or that the revelation should come to me:

1) that the twenty-four Elders themselves were definitely *twenty-four Ancient Worthies* from the ranks of the Old Testament patriarchs and prophets (to include Job and Moses, Joshua and Samuel, and such others) who were "redeemed out of every kindred and tongue and people and nation";

2) that they were initial Firstfruits representing the *Wave Sheaf* (who would be followed fifty days later with other Firstfruits belonging to the same harvest crop and to the same harvest period, represented in the 144,000 who would be constructively *marked* or *sealed* for the purpose of identification) out of the Old Testament Resurrection Harvest which itself was even then ominously imminent. They became redeemed in A.D. 31 as is seen from Matthew 27:50-53, being pegged in the Levitical types to the first day of the Feast of Pentecost;

3) that they were carried to heaven (*where they NOW are!*), being personally escorted thither by Jesus Himself on

the occasion of His First Ascension, in this memorable year of Grace Divine;

4) *that these therefore constituted the very first arrivals of humanity into the Kingdom of God!*

From the foregoing, it was but a further step to the ultimate triumph of divine revelation and grace, expressing as it does *"that which is noted in the Scripture of truth,"* that the resurrection of this Old Testament contingent from their graves at once heralded, and thereby paved the way for, the founding of the glorious *Celestial BODY OF CHRIST* in the selfsame era (namely, the Apostolic Generation) which marked their own redemption. This in turn made it possible for believers in Him and in His Name and in "the Power of His Resurrection," being justified by faith, *thereafter, subsequently, and ever since,* to inherit immortality and celestial glory at the very instant of their mortal dissolution, *this being in fact THE NEW BIRTH, which is the theme and vital message covered in the present Bible study!*

APPENDIX IV

NOTICE

The presentation on *The New Birth* is primarily the outgrowth of certain scriptural studies undertaken in the past, which have generally elicited favorable comment in circles usually well-informed in matters pertaining to God's Word and hence prone in some instances to be a little critical, and in others perhaps even a little hostile, but which in all cases are nevertheless respected. They have all been helpful to me in sending me either to my knees for sustaining strength or, it may be, back to the Word to restudy my subject and come again. On the whole, the reaction has been quite encouraging, and it is this which has thus emboldened the writer into the present attempt.

Among the published studies referred to are the following:

1. *The Harmony of the Resurrection* (a brochure dated Nov., 1929).
2. *The Harmony of the Visits to the Sepulcher* (a monograph dated Feb., 1935).
3. *The Feast of Pentecost* (a monograph dated June, 1954).
4. *Notes on "Te Mia Ton Sabbaton"* (Supplement to "3"—a monograph dated Sept., 1954).

The practical consideration of the foregoing may be necessary in order to grasp the full significance, together with the entire reasoning and logic, of *The New Birth,* as a result of questions left dangling and unresolved in the minds of many who, not being privileged to be acquainted with and examine the above, consequently may still remain perplexed. Perhaps, if the success of *The New Birth* should warrant it by an awakened interest, these studies in a revised form might be assembled together as a separate and distinct publication which would come later. *Let us all hope and pray!*

"Build thee more stately mansions, O my soul,
As the swift seasons roll!
Leave thy low-vaulted past!
Let each new temple, nobler than the last,
Shut thee from heaven with a dome more vast,
Till thou at length art free,
Leaving thine outgrown shell by life's unresting sea!"

—*Oliver Wendell Holmes*
(From "The Chambered Nautilus")

ABOUT THE AUTHOR

CYRIL A. CRICHLOW was born in Trinidad, British West Indies. From his highly religious family he inherited his unquenchable faith as well as his curiosity to probe deeper into the mysteries locked within the Scriptures. At fifteen he was sent to the United States to study at Union College, Nebraska, a missionary institution where he gained the fundamentals of Bible training and evangelism. In 1918 he saw overseas service in France and Germany with the American Expeditionary Forces during World War I.

A government employee since 1927 until his retirement in 1951, Mr. Crichlow has utilized much of his spare time to do research at the Library of Congress. He is an evangelist and Promotion Director for the Christian Fellowship of the World in Washington, D. C.—a legacy which he inherited from the late Professor John Alexander Logan Derby, Ph.D., of West Hartford, Connecticut, on the faculty staff at Union College in Nebraska in former years, and the late Percival J. Laird of Paw Paw, Michigan, one-time Missionary to China from the British Isles.

At various times in his very active and rewarding life he has been a pastor, religious writer, associate editor, court reporter, and co-owner of a business school in New York. His travels have taken him to Liberia on the West Coast of Africa, including a second trip to Europe (this time as a civilian) which enabled him to visit Spain and the fortress of Gibraltar.

Among his previously published works are: *The Harmony of the Resurrection, The Harmony of the Visits to the Sepulcher, The Feast of Pentecost, The Triune Name, The Godhead a Dualism, not a Trinity,* besides many other writings.

In lieu of his picture, Mr. Crichlow writes that he is personally not interested in presenting himself in terms of vanity display but rather in terms of self-effacement. And for this reason he adds the statement: "The message of THE NEW BIRTH strictly embraces the Gospel of salvation as this is completely provided through Jesus Christ the risen and ascended Lord. It therefore seeks to present HIM—as the forerunner distinguished as John the Baptist presented Him—in the following terms: 'He must increase, but I must decrease!'—John 3:30."